CONTENTS

Introduction	1
An Unruly Child	2
Augie	4
Baseball	7
Asteroid	9
Bed Bugs	12
Best Friends	14
Big City	16
Bobby	18
Bobo	21
Brain Damage	23
Camping Trip	25
Car Chasin' Chicken	28
Clary's Pond	29
Common Core	32
Country Preacher	33
Credit Card	35
Dead Battery	37
Death of a Star	39
DOA	42
Doomsday	45

Earl Ray Summers	47
Eldon Cooper	50
Emergence	52
Family Farm	55
Futbol	57
Future House	59
Game Day	61
Ghost Town	63
Going Home	65
Goin' Vegan	67
Harley Slater	68
Hole in the Sky	71
Hunter and Prey	73
Iko Nakamura	75
In Dementia	77
Indian Summer	79
Jenny Lee	82
Job With a View	84
Julie	87
Ladies' Night	89
Livin' Doll	92
Lost Time	95
Magic Beans	98
Mekong River Wine	101
Memory Gardens	104
Missin' You	106
My Back Porch	108
My Cabin	110

My GMC	112
My Prostate	114
Neighbors	115
New Kid	118
Nightmares	120
Not This Child	123
Parole Date	126
Penny Mae	131
Placebo	133
Poor Henry	135
Prison Blues	138
Prison Break	140
Prom Night	142
Radio Flyer	145
Red Cross Kids	147
Requiem for a City	149
Riverboat Gambler	151
Safety Net	154
School Bully	156
Seniors	158
Shadow People	159
Silver Balls	161
Silverback	168
Sitting Bull	170
Soul Train	172
tam biet, Vietnam	175
The Angry Ghost	177
The Boxer	180

The Broken Spoke	181
The Danvers Party	182
The Guardian	195
The Gunfighter	199
The Holidays	202
The Medicine Chest	204
The Old Oak Tree	206
The Plano Posse	209
The Refugee	211
The Starlight	214
The Talisman	216
The Trucker's Wife	219
Thing	221
This Town	224
Time to Die	226
Time Travel	229
Travelin' Jack	231
True Love	252
Turtles and Trains	254
Two Feathers	257
Victory Gardens	264
Weight Loss	266
Wendell Sykes	269
Whistling Rill	271
Who Am I	274
Wild Horses	276
Willa	279
Zero Point Energy	284

Zombies	286
POcket of Time	287
The Linga Wars	295

INTRODUCTION

I have updated this book to add a few new stories, not including *Pocket of Time* and *The Linga Wars*, which are not written using limericks. The rest are indeed written entirely in limericks, but three, *Travelin' Jack*, *Two Feathers* and *The Danvers Party* are written in the style of historical fiction so I have added commentary and narrative in certain places to explain jumps in time and to set historical context.

It was also necessary to add a bit of text to *Silver Balls,* for which the reason will be obvious.

For me, *Pocket of Time* is science fiction and *The Linga Wars* is fantasy but I will leave the reader to decide that.for himself.
                        Bob B.
                        May, 2022

AN UNRULY CHILD

Cedric's parents were happy as can be
They'd waited so long for this delivery
For years they had tried
Then came the surprise
There'll soon be a boy in their nursery

But all was not roses right from the start
Little Cedric cried when they were apart
Nothing could soothe him
So it might behoove them
For one to stay home if the other departs

This seemed to work but just for a while
Apparently, that wasn't Cedric's style
Because soon enough
The boy became tough
Both parents needed for this unruly child

They catered to every wish and demand
Thinking, "This is not what we planned"
"Why do we suffer?"
"Should we be tougher?"
"How will he be when he's a grown man?"

The first few years were a true nightmare
Though Mother and Father tried to be fair
They just couldn't cope
And began to lose hope
As hard as they tried Cedric just didn't care

There's a special camp just for unruly boys
A friend told Dad it would stop all his noise
If you send him out there
They'll shave off his hair
The discipline required is what they employ

Cedric threw a tantrum and refused to go
A counselor trussed him up head to toe
Not the first he'd seen
This retired Marine
Control established without landing a blow

After 3 months of boot camp Cedric returns
Anxious parents wonder what he has learned
Their unruly thug
Greets them with a warm hug
Their baby has done a complete about turn

He tells them about all the things he has done
While away at the camp militarily run
Weapons were taught
Mock battles fought
Whenever his turn came his team always won

To master an art one must practice the drills
At camp Cedric had the most confirmed kills
His Mother's throat cut
A blade in Dad's gut
Cedric feels certain he holds the record still

AUGIE

A storm has been raging throughout the night
Thunderous claps and a sky streaked with light
The fierce driving rain
Shows complete disdain
For anyone daring to face the wind's might

I huddle by the fire to ward off the chill
That crept in my bones and lingers there still
Augie, my pug's
Curled up on the rug
The wind in the rafters is piercing and shrill

A knock on the door shocks Augie awake
Who could be out there, for heaven's sake?
I open the door
And feel the wind's roar
I'm met by a young girl of seven or eight

She says she is lost but how can that be?
There's no one for miles, just Augie and me
I bring her inside
To get herself dried
She sits by the fire and crosses her knees

Augie seems strangely attracted to her
He lays in her lap as she's stroking his fur
He seems so relaxed
In spite of the fact
The little guy is sick, still he doesn't stir

She'll sleep in my big chair close to the fire
I make her hot cocoa and wish to enquire
But her story can wait
'Til the storm abates
We'll talk in the morning and so I retire

Next day she's gone much to my surprise
Maybe she just doesn't care for goodbyes
But no time to fret
We're off to the vet
Augie's due for a checkup and I agonize

He's got a cancer for which there's no cure
Pain's not yet a problem, his vet assures
At least not for now
And I won't allow
Augie to suffer more than he should endure

I tell the vet about the girl at my door
She says there's a story about her and more
But first there is news
The vet is confused
The cancer is gone that was there before

She's never seen cancer just disappear
But there is no doubt, the results are clear
So then she relates
The lost young girl's fate
Mary is the girl who wanders 'round here

Her parents were killed in a violent crash
Mary got out before the car burned to ash
She never was found
Though they searched the grounds
Amid the driving rain and lightning flash

Locals say the child still wanders around
Maybe because Mary's never been found
But one rainy night
She dropped into sight
And sat with a dog who was feeling down

That was ten years ago and Augie is fine
Truth be told, his health is better than mine
Did Mary that night
Put Augie to right?
When I have doubts, he's right here to remind

BASEBALL

If anyone knows of a more boring sport
Than baseball I'd love to see the report
If you are a fan
You won't understand
People like me of the impatient sort

No play clock here to move things along
The only thing timed is the national song
You just have to know
This game is so slow
If you like fast paces then you don't belong

Here's how the play-by-play always goes
After the stretching and warm up throws
The plate umpire calls
"Let's all play ball!"
Is it finally time to start up the show?

The pitcher strides to the pitcher's mound
Adjusts his cap and looks all around
Tugs at his ear
Scratches his rear
Then spits tobacco juice onto the ground

Finally, all of the stars are aligned
So the catcher gives the awaited sign
It's now time to throw
The ball, but oh no
The batter has moved from the spot assigned

He picks up some dirt to rub on his bat
I guess there's a reason he has to do that
With this now complete
He scrapes both his feet
Moves back in the box right after he's spat

This routine repeats itself with every batter
Your time is treated like it doesn't matter
Babysitter must wait
You're gonna be late
Dinner will be eaten on an ice cold platter

Nine times each team will take to the field
Until a winner is finally revealed
But sadly not before
Your bladder is sore
And you don't think your ass will ever heal

We're sad to report the death of a fan
His body is being removed from the stands
The guy met his fate
Too willing to wait
For extra innings as tied scores demand

If you wish to go out and support your team
Take a cushion and some sun block cream
A little NoDoz, too
Might just help you through
There's a reason it's called a field of dreams

ASTEROID

There are constant collisions in the Kuiper Belt
Smashing rocks with the blows they are dealt
A single violent clash
Turns one rock to ash
But the other breaks loose rather than melt

It falls toward the sun due to gravity's pull
Gaining in speed like a mad raging bull
It passes Neptune
And Saturn's big moon
Drawn ever inward a monster quintessential

It's fifty miles long and over thirty miles wide
If it should impact there'll be nowhere to hide
This huge asteroid
Hurtles through the void
With a million tons of iron ore buried inside

Jupiter's gravity greatly increases its velocity
Huge potential energy within this monstrosity
All worlds are now prone
In the goldilocks zone
For it's a planet killer with incredible ferocity

On Earth it's being tracked with telescopes
The initial calculations give reason for hope
It's just a near miss
They're certain of this
A doomsday scenario offers no way to cope

Orbit must be established to enable prediction
Before denying future danger with conviction
It's The Hammer of Thor
No name could suit more
Like a nightmare straight out of science fiction

After many months of careful observation
Computer models show orbital fluctuation
It's shifting its path
'Til Earth feels its wrath
We've seventy-six years until annihilation

Thor is immune to any weapon perceivable
Some believe leaving the planet is conceivable
A far-fetched idea
Or public panacea?
Most think travel to the stars unachievable

But city size ships that could last generations
Drives that provided constant acceleration
Might offer a chance
To cross the expanse
Remaining on Earth would be self-immolation

And so mass production of a radical design
Was begun everywhere to be ready on time
Parts flown into space
Supplying the base
Where huge ships rolled off the assembly line

The people of Earth had forged a new home
In traveling cities with large protective domes
Earth took its last breath
In a fiery death
Its people having said adios and shalom

Their journey continues as the sun fades away
Generations from now their gamble might pay
But will life endure?
No one knows for sure
Just promise each other we'll all see that day

BED BUGS

In the financial district of New York City
Are bars where the girls show off their titties
Behind one of them
Is the Shady Pines Inn
Where folks can get down to the nitty-gritty

The bar is favored by stock traders and guys
Who earn a good living off of sells and buys
Every girl here knows
But for snorting blow
Their favorite pastime is between her thighs

Wall Street Will owns the Shady Pines Inn
It specializes in catering to their whims
Rooms rent by the hour
A short time and shower
Indulging in Sunday's confessional sins

Silicone Susie is just one of the pros
Who can suck a golf ball thru a garden hose
She's a thirty-six D
And lets 'em swing free
There are guys who enjoy that, I suppose

Under each of the beds is a listening device
And Will gives the girls a special low price
To solicit stock tips
On promising blue chips
Then makes a killing on the inside advice

Susie has a boyfriend named Broadway Bob
He's the one who paid for Susie's breast job
And she always comes back
To their rundown old shack
Since hi school he's been Susie's heart throb

They've never been rich although they've tried
Bob's big time cons always have a down side
But now he knows how
To milk a cash cow
In a Shady Pines room his con he'll confide

Soon he's talking about a big deal as planned
The minimum investment is five hundred grand
It's a guaranteed win
For those who get in
He'll double their money once he has it in hand

Susie tells Will he needs cash for this deal
Will says he'll raise it even if he must steal
To get that much dough
Takes a mortgage and so
It requires all Will has but it's finally sealed

Susie and Bob take the money and run
To an unnamed island in the Pacific sun
Soon police find the bugs
A tip from those thugs
And Will is arrested for what he has done

BEST FRIENDS

An old friend of mine just said his goodbye
A long time has passed still I wanted to cry
He's in his dress blues
And those spit-shined shoes
But no fanfare for him, just a regular guy

We met in a bar outside Camp Pendleton
Two young Marines just out having fun
Whatever our fate
It just had to wait
The party would end with the next setting sun

Training was short as the need for new blood
Hurried us through to join up with the flood
Of troops being sent
As reinforcement
For many were dying over there in the mud

We landed together in time for monsoon
First Sergeant assigned us to our new platoon
The place was so wet
A man couldn't get
Dry in a poncho wrapped like a cocoon

They taught us to move in the jungle with care
Charlie leaves booby traps most everywhere
Like sharpened bamboo
Designed to tear through
If you hit the trip wire it'll strip your flesh bare

A night with no moon is a dangerous time
Add in the rain and conditions are prime
They hit us at night
And during the fight
I found myself lying face down in the slime

I tried to get up but my legs wouldn't move
He pulled me upright saying, "I got you, dude!"
I was carried away
How far I can't say
But after a while I began to improve

They sent me back home, my health to restore
We kept up our friendship long after the war
As he's laid to rest
I place on his chest
The Medal of Honor he so proudly wore

BIG CITY

For so many years population increased
More babies born than people deceased
Each one competed
Resources depleted
Many fish netted but few were released

So land was seized driving people away
For huge farms controlled by the USDA
Dairy and grain
Covered the plain
"Move to the city!" was the call of the day

But there's only so much accommodation
The influx created a perilous situation
As things got more dire
They built ever higher
But that didn't help at lower elevations

Moving walkways were built high in the air
Buildings connected by new thoroughfares
Most peoples' feet
Never walk on a street
3-D phone apps guide them everywhere

Monica lives on the ninety-ninth floor
Robots deliver things straight to her door
A little doo-dad
Called an All-in-One Pad
Allows her to order direct from the store

It handles her bills and deposits her pay
And monitors usage of goods day by day
There is no compassion
As all things are rationed
Temptation to spend is held firmly at bay

She works every day and has a boyfriend
But nothing is going the way they intend
Sans government permission
There'll be no addition
For Monica a child would be a godsend

All are sterilized for the good of the state
History demands they control the birthrate
Mothers are chosen
From eggs that were frozen
But Monica's name never got on the slate

An exception may be made if one applies
For reversal procedures that can fertilize
But the council in town
Has flat turned her down
There's just no consoling her as she cries

Out on the balcony as her boyfriend sleeps
She curses this city of mindless sheep
Things look so small
As she starts her fall
First time she's ever encountered a street

BOBBY

Bobby's fifteen as the new school year starts
He's short for his age but strong in his heart
Muscular as well
From lifting dumbbells
All thru the summer he's trained for the part

So he can play football and win for his school
Promising his Mom he would follow the rules
"Don't hurt anyone,
just try to have fun.
You can't lose your temper and act like a fool."

He tries out for the team the very first day
Assuring the coach, he will always obey
But the coach is skeptic
As Bobby' epileptic
He decides to give him a chance anyway

Practice goes well and Bobby's really strong
His teammates like him and they get along
He plows thru the line
Every single time
At defensive tackle is where he belongs

As time goes by, he gets better each day
Until he has a seizure on the field of play
He's flat on his back
Body being wracked
Shaking and convulsing like a sickly ballet

His mother is called once Bobby recovers
One incident's enough, to prevent another
The coach's decision
Despite team division
Is Bobby can't play and informs his mother

Bobby's heartbroken but he understands
Coach is right but Bobby still has his fans
Someone else must sack
The other quarterback
Being a spectator is not what was planned

Nevertheless, Bobby attends every game
Cheering his teammates always by name
He waits on the bench
For the Gatorade drench
Winners or losers, they get wet all the same

They're at an away game on a Friday night
The fans in the bleachers jump with delight
As their hero scores
They shout out, "Two more!"
Then the seating collapses, folding up tight

It buckles in the middle and forms a big "V"
Many fans are pinned as others run to see
Those trapped are crying
While others are trying
To move the huge girders, unsuccessfully

Then Bobby jumps into the tangled wreck
Hands to one side, the other to his back
He pushes the "V"
And it moves gradually
Suddenly he's hit with an epileptic attack

Still, he pushes until the steel moves again
And a chance at rescue is finally attained
Their memory burns bright
Of how Bobby died that night
Even his big heart couldn't take the strain

BOBO

We first met that dog on a hot summer day
Lost and confused and clearly a stray
No collar or tag
But his tail sure could wag
The look in his eyes said, "Please let me stay!"

Jeremy, our son, who was six at the time
Lived in a world that was his but not mine
Autism, they say
Takes our children away
And search as you may you never will find

Blankies could hold him but not Mom or Dad
Only something soft so he'd be gently clad
"Oh, what have we done
that we can't touch our son?"
But there is no answer no matter how sad

We let that stray dog into our back yard
To feed him but we had to be on our guard
We couldn't foresee
How Jeremy might be
If he saw a creature so motley and scarred

He ran to the window and flashed a big grin
Jumped up and down saying, "Bobo, it's him!"
He's talking, you see
About a dog on TV
Now he was Bobo as though he always had been

We cleaned Bobo up and allowed him inside
He went right to Jeremy and laid down beside
With a boy's arm around
And his soft breathing sound
Content with his lot he just heaved a big sigh

In time our relationship with Jeremy changed
We felt him becoming much less estranged
While Bobo was there
Laughter filled the air
Clinging to each other hugs were exchanged

But no living creature stays forever young
Each of our songs' final verse must be sung
For Bobo it came
As a peaceful refrain
But Jeremy's life was becoming unstrung

Slowly our son drew back into his shell
The world he first knew became a fresh hell
Without his best friend
On whom to depend
He drifted away in a final farewell

Heartbreak can't kill you most people will say
Yet it took our sweet Jeremy one Winter's Day
But some happiness was
In his brief life because
A stray he named Bobo once came our way

BRAIN DAMAGE

Lester is not the brightest bulb on the tree
A heart of gold and good intentions has he
Just a regular Joe
Like you and I know
Friendly to everyone he happens to see

He works on a loading dock 8 hours a day
Moving large pallets from shipboard to quay
Guiding them down
From the ship to the ground
Rope and his muscles controlling its sway

But one day a pallet escaped from his grip
Sending it falling from the deck of the ship
It hit Lester square
Where ear meets with hair
Requiring an emergency ambulance trip

When Lester arrived at the Emergency Room
All saw the poor guy as certainly doomed
Unconscious and swollen
His life surely stolen
But each did his best in spite of the gloom

Lester wasn't done and lived thru the night
He didn't awaken but continued to fight
Although he was weak
He was trying to speak
An unconscious thought was seeking the light

A nurse leaned in closer in an effort to hear
His lips ever nearer her inquisitive ear
"What you must do
is stop 5-4-2!"
What possible meaning a message so queer?

Several times many others heard as well
The quizzical message was clear as a bell
But what did it mean?
Perhaps just a dream
By a man grossly injured when that pallet fell

When Lester woke up after noon the next day
Everyone hoped that he might be okay
When told he had spoken
Before he'd awoken
Poor confused Lester asked, "What did I say?"

The message repeated made no sense at all
The last thing recalled was the big pallet's fall
The swelling's decreased
So Lester's released
If he has any problem be certain to call

He cheerfully returns to his job the next day
Guiding the pallets down onto the quay
But is Lester aware
that Northwestern Air
flight 5-4-2 just crashed in the bay?

CAMPING TRIP

My son turned ten and I had a surprise
A weekend of camping for just us 2 guys
I will teach my child
The ways of the wild
Living with nature under starlit skies

To outfit our trip the best possible way
I went to Bass Pro the following day
My money well spent
On a nice 2-man tent
Instructions are easy-to-follow, they say

So Saturday morning we're off to the lake
TV and internet get a much-needed break
Relax for a while
Go camping in style
See how many catfish we're able to take

We settled on a spot down close to the shore
Laid down our gear and set to our chores
Firewood to collect
A tent to erect
Junior gathers kindling from the forest floor

Assembling this tent is a puzzle to me
Tab J doesn't fit into Slot Twenty-Three
And the forward pole
Is missing its hole
Where in the world is Floor Panel Seven-C?

At last it's together though it leans to one side
I guess it will do and store supplies inside
Now I am itching
To do some fishing
We go to catch supper grinning with pride

After three long hours I'm near comatose
The only thing biting are the damn mosquitos
Now Junior has a rash
From his feet to his ass
He got Poison Oak in the woods, I suppose

If that wasn't enough, it's starting to rain
My boy looks at me and says, "Never again!"
"Let's get out of here!"
So we snatch up our gear
We head back to the tent, there to remain

But all my hard work is lying on the ground
Food and their wrappers are tossed all around
Then out of nowhere
A monstrous black bear
Comes charging at us making terrible sounds

In my haste to get out I bumped into a tree
Causing an attack by a huge swarm of bees
The trip was a bust
And So in disgust
We ate Saturday's supper at Chuck E. Cheese

Sunday is spent treating Poison Oak and stings
Feeling the relief that soothing lotion brings
My son hates my guts
The wife thinks I'm nuts
So what do they know about doing man things?

I'm here in the garage with a six-pack of beer
In spite of it all, I am still of good cheer
My boy may be mad
But he's like his dad
One day he'll be sitting with me right out here

CAR CHASIN' CHICKEN

I once had a chicken that liked to chase cars
It would run like the devil but never got far
Returned in disgust
Its efforts a bust
Crushing the dreams of the poultry track star

One day a huge truck rolled by on the road
It came to a grade so the big semi slowed
And that angry pullet
Took off like a bullet
In spite of past failures, it set out unbowed

A hundred yards later it closed on its prey
Determined that this time it won't get away
But it ran out of luck
When it caught that truck
With the KFC logo proudly displayed

CLARY'S POND

Henry and Rebecca had just recently wed
And staked out a parcel as their homestead
"It's Clary land now!"
They solemnly vowed
"And so it shall be 'til the Clary's are dead."

Rebecca gave birth to a boy they adored
The land and their name will be his reward
Through tears and laughter
Clary's thereafter
Made proud use of all the land would afford

A hundred years later the land was sill theirs
Jonas and Myra ran the Clary affairs
Our house was nearby
And I wasn't shy
We didn't have fences or signs to beware

When I first met her, I was nine years old
I called her Miss Myra as I had been told
She knew I was fond
Of their fishing pond
It had just about all the fish it could hold

Times then were hard; we had little to eat
Fish from the pond were a welcome treat
With cornbread and greens
It gave us the means
To a proper supper before a sound sleep

As I grew up Miss Myra lost her smile
I later would learn she couldn't bear a child
The second world war
And Army Air Corps
Took 4 years from me and in the meanwhile

Miss Myra had died, from TB people said
And Jonas was broken but he wasn't dead
Kept working the land
With just his two hands
To bring in the crop he hired helpers instead

Jonas grew old and it wouldn't be long
Before the last Clary would sing a sad song
"I can't leave a son
to see the work done."
But still he hung on and tried to be strong

Soon Jonas was held to his bed every day
Unable to work but he didn't dismay
The crop still fared well
Until time to sell
The land took care of itself in some way.

At last Jonas passed and no Clary's remained
The pond became stagnant; fish not sustained
Crops withered and died
No matter they tried
Life that had been in the land was now drained

The place went for auction but it never sold
Folks around here didn't need to be told
It's no use to plow
The land won't allow
Any but a Clary to work their freehold

Now 40 years gone come the end of May
Those who still remember have this to say,
"It's all for the best,
the land is at rest;
it waits for a Clary to return some day."

COMMON CORE

I'm a mathematical kind of a guy
I like tangents and cosines and pi
I feel right at home
With a calculus tome
Differential equations, "Oh my!"

A new kind of math I've been told
Is replacing the methods of old
So I thought I would try
The new multiply
Would I fit in the Common Core mold?

After laying out boxes in rows
To see how the end product grows
The multiplicand
Was not where I planned
Why any would use this, who knows?

COUNTRY PREACHER

An old country preacher stopped by today
Says he can save me if only I'll pray
The first thought I got
Is save me from what?
I don't see no trouble a headin' my way

Seems I'm a sinner and going to hell
I wonder out loud just how he can tell
He says he can see
By lookin' at me
The scars of my past and my future as well

I make my own whiskey; I gamble and drink
The devil is here and I'm right on the brink
He'll bury my soul
In his fiery hole
I won't see it comin', he's quick as a wink

But the cost of salvation is too much for me
Give up the things I enjoy to be free?
Can't pay the rent
But tithe ten per cent?
If you want forgiveness you must pay the fee

This rickety shack on the mountain is mine
I'll stay here and keep on a makin' my shine
It's here I reside
My jug by my side
Ol' Satan can join me and drink of my wine

Now parson you know I don't bear you no ill
You're on your own path and follow it still
But yours ain't my way
So all I can say
Is you and your gospels get offa my hill

CREDIT CARD

How many of them have we thrown away?
Those credit card company letters that say
We have great new rates
So don't hesitate
Fill out the form and send it in today

So I do as they ask and stick it in the mail
Only to find that my efforts have failed
I'm just a bit shy
And don't qualify
For Platinum rates but it's a minor detail

Enclosed is a card they've sent me for free
If I will try it, they're sure I will see
It's so easy to use
Need a new pair of shoes?
It's simple and convenient they guarantee

So I sign on the back, see no reason to stall
Jump in the car and go straight to the mall
'Cause I'm anxious to try
Stream fishing with a fly
And I do need new hunting gear for the Fall

Speaking of fishing, I could use a bass boat
I'd like to sail the lake in something that floats
I'll need camping gear
A good supply of beer
Come Winter a warm hat and big overcoat

I charge all of that and head on back home
Turn on the network that lets you shop alone
I charge a few things
'Cause I ain't got no bling
Then I list it on eBay, prices cut to the bone

They think that I'm stupid because I pay rent
Can't afford to buy as my money's all spent
So they can get away
With making me pay
Monthly interest rates of over forty percent

I didn't have no credit before they found me
And I won't have none later, just wait and see
But in the meantime
It's all on their dime
What money I get will be mine and tax free

I'll sell what I bought for cents on the dollar
When they can't recoup, I'll listen to 'em holler
But that bit of cash
Goes into my stash
And bankruptcy'll get 'em hot under the collar

I'll end up no worse than I ever was before
They'll be payin' the bills from the stores
If they're feeling bitter
They might reconsider
And not send free offers to people anymore

DEAD BATTERY

Must find a charger, phone has gone dead
Friends are still texting; what have they said?
The meeting's at noon
But I don't have Zoom
If I don't attend it will cost me my head

There's a man with a tablet sitting nearby
I'll borrow his charger if he will comply
But as I draw near
It soon becomes clear
A book, not a tablet has captured his eye

He looks up and smiles, then says "Hello"
Most people don't notice wherever I go
I wave as I pass
Eyes fixed on the grass
No time to engage as I'm late for the show

Hurry on to the office to attend in person
Really don't want my situation to worsen
My boss looks at me
Surprised as can be
Surrounded by monitor images conversin'

We are the only ones physically present
All of the others are virtual attendants
Coffee and pastries
Look very tasty
But the air in the room is mostly unpleasant

A new assistant manager is to be selected
Now that everyone is finally connected
We're not here to vote
The boss will promote
But not who the rest of us had expected

"Since only one of you thought it useful
to be here in person I'll be brutally truthful."
"A manager must be
here for all to see;
leading from the front is absolutely crucial."

So I get a promotion by sheer accident
The dead battery was just a coincidence
I can't tell anyone
Or my new job is done
Monday I must take over in any event

When I go in, I won't know what to do
I've had no experience in leading a crew
I'm sure I'll fall flat
There's no doubt of that
Taunting and laughing is bound to ensue

Back in the park he gives me the same look
The man is still reading; he has stayed put
Another hello
He smiles and I know
I'll stop at the library and pick up a book

DEATH OF A STAR

Tommie Lee came from a small Texas town
Left little behind but the dirt on the ground
Set out for Nashville
Where stars are made still
He'd just a guitar and his own country sound

Saloons you can play in line Music Row
To launch a career that's where you must go
There's no guarantee
As many soon see
But Tommie's determined to star in the show

Night after night he earns nickels and dimes
But he's not discouraged, just biding his time
The audience cheers
And sends him free beers
Which Tommie believes is a positive sign

One night a record producer gets a call
Come see this kid with the soft Texas drawl
He plays by himself
Like nobody else
If you're looking for talent this boy's got it all

So Tommie Lee Barber's career then began
Producer wants backup so hires him a band
Steel guitar and bass
But Tommie's the face
They'll see on the billboards all over the land

The Red River Boys, as they took for a name
Sold out in Nashville wherever they came
Women and booze
They had but to choose
But you must go on tour to really gain fame

From TV to stadium the audience was floored
The Red River Boys became nationally adored
But the road is so long
To continue their song
Many pills taken and Jack Daniels poured

Some pills got him up and others let him down
That's how it went then, around and around
He starts missing dates
The producer's irate
Tommie's boxed in as though he might drown

Fickle is fame and for some there's no joy
That's how it turned out for our Tommie boy
Even the innocent
Find that they're impotent
Drugs and the booze in the end will destroy

Tommie's final gig was in Madison Square
Thousands of people had bought tickets there
But he didn't go
So they cancelled the show
Their star was long gone and no one knew where

Tommie now plays in the halls of the subway
Nickels and dimes once again are his pay
The same old guitar
That made him a star
Is all he has left from those glorious days

A few recognize him and sneer with disdain
In the pit of his stomach is a sickening pain
Just one final fix
For the boy from the sticks
And he steps in front of the underground train

DOA

The Dead On Arrival Funeral Home
Is as close to you as your telephone
We make you look great
As you lie in state
Promotions on caskets and granite headstones

The business had been in the family for years
Folks were still dying but one thing was clear
Those fancy last rites
When money is tight
Make way for more frugal ways to shed tears

Urns are much cheaper than coffins and so
Cremation's becoming the new way to go
A body and sheet
Just turn up the heat
Grampa's up there with the mantle's photos

The County has always paid for cremations
So few Potter's Fields are left in the nation
The fixed price they pay
Is the same today
As it was years ago, no account for inflation

Their books are awash with red ink today
How long they might last nobody can say
Inventory is low
With business so slow
But building and contents all have been paid

A family meeting is held to decide
How we can help our business survive
If something's not done
We've nowhere to run
All we'll be able to say is we tried

Jimmy was always a kind of black sheep
Wont to make promises he couldn't keep
But his big idea
To see their way clear
Holds lots of promise but it won't be cheap

We'll convert the furnace to a barbecue grill
Put a pizza oven on one end, as well
The idea's the same
Just turn down the flame
We're already zoned as a business to sell

A dining room where the loved ones once sat
To mourn the deceased and quietly chat
Tables were added
Chairs were re-padded
A tile floor replaced the old carpets and mats

They held a grand opening one summer day
People were hesitant so some stayed away
It was, after all
A funeral hall
But word got around it was well worth the pay

For seventy years bodies burned back there
Everyone knows it but nobody cares
The pizzas and steaks
Have such a great taste
And the smell of cooking smoke fills the air

The family considers their success a big win
Bills are all paid and the money flows in
Of course, there are still
Requests to fulfill
So they must serve the county now and again

DOOMSDAY

A world beset by devastation
Forced a mass evacuation
And into space
Began the race
To find a safe new habitation

A world of green and blue they found
Their feet upon most fertile ground
Just standing still
To move no will
Enraptured by both sight and sound

Creatures fly and some climb trees
Seedlings floating in the breeze
And one that moves
On just two hooves
Much as they do and with ease

But this place of beauty is not for them
To remain here surely would condemn
This curious being
First time seeing
They who almost look like him

What lay in store no one can say
But why not help them on their way
A single strand
From hand to hand
As lost in sleep they peaceful lay

And so time passes as it must
Changes happen and they adjust
Soon tools are made
And they begin to trade
Clans are formed on bonds of trust

Soon thereafter the seas are being sailed
Telephones are ringing and letters mailed
But soon enough
Things are getting tough
And political dissidents are being jailed

Men have now learned to hate their own
Coveting things their friends have sown
With new weapons out
They flaunt their clout
'Cuz the biggest dog always gets the bone

Several countries now have the means
To blow the Earth to smithereens
The latest news
They've lit the fuse
An end the others had not foreseen

They'd hoped to nudge us on our way
So they could return again one day
But their bequest
Has only left
The remnants of their own doomsday

EARL RAY SUMMERS

Earl Ray grew up on the Summers' farm
He and his Daddy raised up the new barn
A big lad was he
Standing six feet three
But Earl Ray would never do anyone harm

No time for school with chores to be done
When he was just ten his Daddy said "Son,
the farm needs you here
most days of the year,
and learning to farm is best in the long run."

So Earl Ray had none of the social graces
One usually acquires when visiting places
Where manners are learned
And respect is earned
Mingling with others in community spaces

He was 30 years old when his Daddy died
His Mom followed soon and buried beside
The farm thus conveyed
To orphan Earl Ray
How will he manage with no one to guide?

Maybe he can find some assistance in town
So he saddled a horse and trotted on down
He wasn't quite sure
What to look for
But figured he'd know it once it was found

It was late in the day when he saw the saloon
No harm in stopping, it was well past noon
Earl Ray had drunk shine
But just a few times
Daddy bought a jug once in a blue moon

He'd stop for one drink after such a long day
A painted lady spots him from a mile away
She walks up and smiles
Bids him stay a while
Her name is Lacy, he replies "I'm Earl Ray."

She drinks as much as he but holds it well
Soon he's telling the story of his fresh hell
She'll sympathize
As long as he buys
That's her job, you know, to listen and sell

Earl Ray is a rube and she's seen so many
Over the years she's taken them for plenty
Now this guy comes in
So down in the chin
He's asking to be fleeced for every penny

Soon the bartender flashes her the evil eye
Drinking has slowed, that's the reason why
Earl Ray's had his fill
And smells like a still
So he says it's high time he said good-bye

Lacy says she doesn't want to see him go
She likes this big farm boy and tells him so
"Then come home with me!"
And Lacy agrees
Instinct is telling her to see where this goes

It's morning and Lacy is bright-eyed awake
Sitting upright she gives Earl Ray a shake
In spite of the drink
She knows he don't think
The work on the farm will give him a break

He's up in a flash and throws Lacy a look
That she understands like opening a book
There's love in his eyes
That can't be disguised
He laughs when he asks her if she can cook

Breakfast is ready and Earl Ray sits down
Bacon is crisp and the biscuits are brown
There's fried eggs and ham
And strawberry jam
Even Lacy is proud as she looks around

Earl Ray and Lacy are still finding their way
An unlikely pair who found love on that day
A proud farmer's son
Who wouldn't hurt anyone
And a barroom hustler who just walked away

ELDON COOPER

The Coopers mined coal for six generations
Then came Obama with his new regulations
Mines began closing
Superimposing
Poverty on an already poor population

Drugs found their way into coal country then
Proud men no longer could care for their kin
So sank to a low
No one thought they'd go
Life would never be the way it had been

Eldon remembered the things he'd been told
That moonshine has value like silver or gold
So he took to the hills
And set up his still
The family raised corn but it never was sold

Moonshine was peddled but outside of town
In case ATF should come sneaking around
But folks here are smart
Take privacy to heart
One nosy outsider would shut the still down

For years Eldon Cooper got by on his shine
Hoping that soon they'd reopen the mines
But the government curse
Just kept getting worse
'Til at last he was selling across the state line

What he's now doing is a federal offense
For which Eldon hasn't any legal defense
His children are crying
But the judge isn't buying
He lectures Eldon from his seat on the bench

The sentence is harsh, 20 years in the can
His family devastated at the loss of their man
How can this be?
Can't the judge see
the misery caused by the government's plan?

Famine and hardship are now a way of life
Appalachia has never experienced such strife
But the new President
Has said he'll relent
And cut regulations with his executive knife

True to his word he has rolled them all back
And mine operations are getting on track
Workers returning
New coal oil burning
But the Coopers still suffer in a 1-room shack

Obama gave pardons on his way out the door
Forgiving drug crimes, conspiracy and more
Criminals went back
To selling their crack
While Eldon still paces a cold prison floor

EMERGENCE

The sky is dark thought it's mid-time of day
With burning ash swirling every which way
Hunters of the clan
Now far from their land
Are caught unawares while out on foray

The familiar mountain with peak now aglow
Has in the past been a good place to go
With plentiful game
But this burning rain
Has them confused and they're suffering so

We'll call him Dregg though he has no name
And the clan has no leader but just the same
Many look to him
When confusion sets in
He seems to know things that they can't explain

He sees a cave very near where they stand
And runs into it with some grass in his hands
He catches some embers
Because he remembers
A fire can be made if the embers are fanned

Protected from the burning rain in the cave
Dregg adds some splinters in an effort to save
The fire he has made
With just a few blades
Danger from animals in this firestorm is grave

The fire is maintained and a full day is spent
Waiting for the mountain to finish its vent
Next morning it's clear
But they find little cheer
Returning empty handed was not the intent

His mate should greet him but she isn't there
Others tell Dregg that she's gone to where
The young ones are birthed
And left to the earth
If they survive overnight, they'll be given care

Next day Dregg returns with his new baby boy
Now is the time to be filled with great joy
But even his supporters'
Tempers grow shorter
Infighting is something they've tried to avoid

Some who are jealous of Dregg and his mate
Blame the failed hunt on not willing to wait
In spite of the flames
There must have been game
Dregg is the cause of the clan's starving state

His enemies kill him saying he must atone
For leading the hunt empty handed back home
His mate's filled with grief
But sorrow is brief
For now she is left to raise Drogg on her own

Somehow the clan has managed to survive
Thanks to his mother Drogg was able to thrive
He keeps to himself
While everyone else
Secretly wishes that Dregg was still alive

The blood of his father runs thru Drogg's veins
He camouflages traps to capture wild game
His nets cleverly
Pull fish from the sea
He seeks not to lead lest his efforts inflame

In time he will father children of his own
They too will inherit the seed Dregg has sown
No one could subvert
This thinking growth spurt
That it occurred is a fact widely known

A new kind of human had recently appeared
One that the others would soon learn to fear
A void had been filled
The things they would build
Would reshape the world in the coming years

Cities would rise where once had been sand
Agriculture soon would crisscross the land
And maybe Dregg knew
That armies come too
It's no fault of his as wisdom's unplanned

FAMILY FARM

I was raised on a farm with my whole family
Mama and Papa, five siblings and me
We ate what we grew
And all of us knew
A better way of life there just couldn't be

We rose long before the sun melts the dew
Did all of our chores and when we were thru
Fried eggs and ham
Biscuits and jam
Then out to the fields, much work still to do

Weekdays we kids went down to the road
To let the yellow school bus lighten our load
But our work would wait
'Til we walked thru the gate
Hogs to be fed and new hay to be mowed

One day the government came to our land
New regulations they held in their hands
Now we can' raise
The one crop that pays
'Cause too much supply reduces demand

They'll buy up our land if we're willing to sell
All of our neighbors were told this as well
Farm corporations
Are sweeping the nation
With no crop to harvest not much left to tell

My brothers and sisters and I moved away
But Mama and Papa are there to this day
They don't work the plow
And all you'll see now
Are 2 wooden crosses that mark where they lay

FUTBOL

What the Hell happened to American men?
They're just not the same as way back when
Guys fought the big war
Gave Hitler what for
With swarthy good looks and a rock-solid chin

Now some wear pink and use pronouns to suit
Live with their parents 'til they get the boot
They march for their rights
But too scared to fight
If called to defend us would they even shoot?

European influence is squarely to blame
It made its way into our Friday night games
Injuries sustained
So Mothers complained
While their sons were dreaming of NFL fame

They told our young men that soccer is a sport
Made them wear stockings and little silk shorts
They called it futbol
Confusing us all
It sounded the same but was nothing of the sort

It doesn't resemble the game we once played
To call it a sport is a brazen charade
Kick a little ball
Use no hands at all
And physical contact must never be made

They say the rest of the world plays futbol
That may be the case but do they recall
When the world went to hell
And most of Europe fell
We Yanks were the ones who answered the call

We may have soccer moms and minivans
But there are still young boys who understand
That a few hard knocks
Don't bother real jocks
And getting back up is what makes one a man

So take little Susie to soccer practice
Without her iPhone so she'll remain active
Leave Johnny alone
To decide on his own
Let's not allow the Europeans to distract us

FUTURE HOUSE

Lacy and Jake live a fast-paced lifestyle
Upwardly mobile their millennial profile
They've hectic careers
Keeping up with their peers
The new home was costly albeit worthwhile

With full automation it does all the chores
VaccuBot mops up and sweeps all the floors
Every room is polled
For temperature control
There's biometric entry on all of the doors

Coffee is ready as soon as they wake
Latte for Lacy and espresso for Jake
They program their meals
On a robot with wheels
They don't have to cook, let AutoChef make

House is controlled by Wi-Fi automation
MasterFridge's brain is the CPU station
Grocery orders based
On each of their tastes
Deliveries concluded without participation

All of their data is stored in the cloud
Tampering with it was never allowed
Until someone hacked
And quietly attacked
Through House's data they silently plowed

Little things happened at first that annoyed
Like VaccuBot carelessly failing to avoid
The leg of a table
Which loudly enabled
A bottle of wine to be completely destroyed

Mistakes then occurred with service of food
Lighting no longer set according to mood
They tried to complain
To the maker in vain
And that's when catastrophe truly ensued

MasterFridge no longer accepting commands
Meals don't arrive in response to demands
The heat is twofold
Shower water is cold
Cyber revenge is the end that's been planned

Lacy and Jake are confined there within
Prisoners in House on a MasterFridge whim
Their cell phones are blocked
Doors and windows locked
Bulletproof glass is now keeping them in

House now accepts all incoming phone calls
Its synthesized voice simulating Jake's drawl
Forget the rat race
They're in a worse place
Trapped until death within digital walls

GAME DAY

Tommy Curtis is the leader of the pack
He's the one who coordinates attacks
Code name Striker-One
He's the fastest gun
Runs in charging as the others lay back

They play every day after school online
No time to do what the teacher assigned
You must hone your skills
To get the most kills
No time for calculus, gotta plan the crime

A nerd named Harold was at the start of it
But shooting and killing is at the heart of it
So when he said no
Harold had to go
That candy ass didn't want any part of it

The online game is just a practice drill
A rehearsal for the most glorious kill
A school assembly
Will be most unfriendly
The massacre will be the greatest thrill

There are ten of them in Stryker's platoon
He knows that Game Day is coming soon
They have to prepare
For the coming warfare
So drills must be practiced every afternoon

Driller's a mean one and won't fool around
His dad owns a gun shop outside of town
Once it's all clear
They load up on gear
AK's, Kevlar vests and hundreds of rounds

Those rich snot-nosed little mommy's boys
Will shit their pants when we bring our toys
They'll watch as their blood
Pours into the mud
And cover their ears to shut out the noise

But Harold has never forgotten the code
He follows their progress in passive mode
As he sees their design
It's clear in his mind
The carnage their operation could bode

Harold has notified the law of the attack
Let them handle this, he's gonna stay back
The cops lie in wait
And they're met at the gate
Stryker's team has been truly bushwhacked

All raise their hands except Stryker-One
His men have deserted and now he is done
He aims at a cop
And is quickly dropped
The only casualty of the war he'd begun

GHOST TOWN

Broken Wheel, Nevada was a gold mining town
Hundreds poured in to pull ore from the ground
As each strike was made
Others came to trade
On the frailties of those whom fortune had found

Saloons and bawdy houses crowded the street
Gambling devices all were programmed to cheat
At the end of the day
Miners wanted to play
Card sharks and painted ladies anxious to meet

Watered down whiskey kept everyone loose
A wide awake gambler just wasn't much use
But once lubricated
Their money liberated
The taking was just like the fabled golden goose

It continued like that for several wild years
Some went home wealthy but most left in tears
At last time to go
With nothing to show
The gold had played out as everyone feared

Thomas McReady was a cautious young man
Who worked his claim as well as anyone can
Keeping most of the gold
An what little he sold
Was just for supplies to survive in this land

No gambler was he and spoke not of his wealth
In that lawless town it was bad for one's health
The only assayer
Was not a fair player
He paid less than fair price from his money belt

Tom moved back home when he'd got his share
The Tennessee hills and his girl waited there
He bought a plot of land
Raised a cabin by hand
And invited their kin who came from everywhere

As Tom and his new wife continued to meet
Folks who had traveled a long way to greet
Broken Wheel went bust
Fell into the dust
Only the tumbleweeds now populate the street

GOING HOME

When I was a boy in my old neighborhood
Doors weren't locked and it was understood
If you needed a cup
We'd fill you right up
Everyone who borrowed always made good

Twenty cents for gas and a nickel for a coke
We didn't have a lot but nobody was broke
On a hot summer day
The little ones play
A wet slip-and-slide invites the breast stroke

Evening came around and we rolled out the grill
Sweet tea and hot dogs, we all ate our fill
Fireflies in jars
Under the stars
Swatting mosquitoes swooping in for the kill

A Sears Craftsman mower we had in the shed
Was my pride and joy 'cause I got it on cred
Dad had cosigned
Said, "Don't fall behind!'
Many lawns mowed to get out of the red

The neighbor's dog barked but he never bit
A big bluff he was and that's the truth of it
When he grew old and died
All us boys cried
But in front of each other none would permit

Suddenly high school was over for me
And I had no plans for what was to be
A few good men needed
And so, I conceded
Four years a Marine just might be the key

A military life lived for so many years
Now it is over and time to switch gears
But first a short break
For I feel I must make
A quick visit home before that career

Friends that I knew have left here for good
A 7 Eleven where our old house once stood
No joy have I found
On my old stomping ground
Nothing's the same in my old neighborhood

GOIN' VEGAN

I'm a true carnivore, eat most any red meat
Potatoes and gravy make the repast complete
A little red wine
Whenever I dine
Then gout hits my joints and turns to concrete

So I go to the doctor who provides me advice
If I drink lots of water it won't crystallize
Ten glasses a day
Will keep gout away
Unfortunately, my bladder is not the right size

Between lots of water and a huge prostate
I get little sleep but can't stay in bed late
I've too much to do
Must stay close to the loo
Being tired makes me dizzy and hallucinate

Now I look like I've been thru an earthquake
The final straw was the golf cart in the lake
The steak and the wine
Caused my health to decline
I'm gonna go vegan before everything breaks!

HARLEY SLATER

Harley Slater was a US Marine
Who never suffered from low self esteem
Until he returned
With third degree burns
From an exploding truckload of gasoline

A tanker had just left the motor pool
When a Taliban round hit its cargo of fuel
The new Kevlar vest
Protected his chest
But the engulfing fireball couldn't be fooled

A fellow Marine threw a tarp over him
It put out the fire but the outlook was grim
His head, hands and arms
Absorbed the most harm
Many thought his chance of survival slim

He's flown to Germany's Ramstein Air Base
The hospital there began treating his face
They did what they could
But it didn't look good
They sent him back to the United States

At Walter Reed there were many skin grafts
And painful recovery as time slowly passed
A blissful sensation
While under sedation
Then he wakes up to the dismal forecast

Return to Afghanistan denied permission
He can't stay in the Corps in his condition
Where else can he go?
People turn away so
He decides to hoard his VA prescription

They give him opioids to deal with the pain
But it hurts less and less and so he refrains
When he has enough
Of that killer stuff
He'll see himself out on the overdose train

They can't repair the scars from the burns
My life is my own and no one's concern
Jack Daniels, my friend
Will do 'til the end
When I go out it will be on my terms

Harley was on his third or fourth double
When a soft voice said, "You seem troubled"
"I'm troubled, you think?"
He said to his drink
Using his sleeve to wipe a five-day stubble

"If you look at my face and don't turn away,
you must be blind so you're welcome to stay.
But I'm bad company,
even though you can't see,
my troubles, like yours, remain every day."

"Yes, I am blind", the gentle voice replied.
"Whether it's trouble is for me to decide."
He thought for a bit
Then had to admit
Acceptance has helped her put worry aside

"Much I have done may require forgiving.
That doesn't mean I have any misgivings.
A man's life is his
and the truth of it is
death is just your punishment for living."

"Then do all you can for the time you're here.
Don't waste any of it by crying in your beer.
It's time I must go
but a thought for the road:
Why not think of your scars as souvenirs?"

He told the bartender when she said goodbye
"That blind girl made sense so I'm gonna try."
He replied, "Well, OK,
but it's a slow day.
There's been no one here beside us two guys."

HOLE IN THE SKY

This dim frigid world is in perpetual night
Its stark frozen surface diffuses the light
Large bulbous eyes
Help these creatures survive
Under the ice they rely on their sight

Here in the ocean they're born and they die
Not knowing what lies up above the thick sky
One day the light rose
Just a bit but for those
Close to the source it was harsh on the eyes

A hole had appeared in the ice overhead
But soon a strange object filled it instead
Shiny and smooth
It's able to move
As a spinning device pushes it straight ahead

Only a god could perform such a feat
So all who were there attempted to meet
But straight down it went
In a rapid descent
To the hard pack below landing on metal feet

Soon it returns rising up toward the light
Many swim around it in childish delight
They beg it to stay
But soon it's away
Back through the hole it continues its flight

Its exit pulls some of the creatures along
Swirling hoarfrost sings a most deadly song
But those left behind
See this action as kind
How could their pass into heaven be wrong?

The hole freezes over in a very short time
They fashion an altar carved into the rime
A simple device
Drills a hole in some ice
And a childlike population believes it divine

A god takes a few but the others are spurned
Perhaps there's a lesson in that to be learned
Whatever the case
In the cold depths of space
The world of Europa awaits its return

HUNTER AND PREY

The moon's a faint crescent in the night sky
Rose from the horizon as though it could fly
On dark night like this
It's easy to miss
A wraith in the darkness as it draws ever nigh

The shadowy figure journeys thru the night
A grey mist has risen and suffuses the light
He's driven by need
And soon he must feed
But care must be taken to stay out of sight

Men have reviled him for hundreds of years
Projecting onto him the sum of their fears
He kills to survive
As does any alive
Never for sport as do his frail human peers

For six hundred years he's avoided the fate
That so long ago had befallen his mate
The hunter had found
Her burial mound
Ending her life with a sharp wooden stake

He's the last of his kind as far as he knows
And the Hunter follows wherever he goes
It's much older than he
And is able to see
Into the darkness and through the shadows

The Hunter's a warlock a thousand years old
How many he's killed may not ever be told
But this one's the last
Then the Hunter may pass
Through the Great Gate into eternity's fold

He's entered the mind of a wolf in the wild
Leader of its pack which is now reconciled
To obey his thoughts
This capture unsought
They're now his familiars, their free will exiled

For centuries past this battle's been foretold
Where good must face evil and so it unfolds
He's high in a cave
With crossbow and stave
His mind calls the wolf to his stronghold

He waits 'til the Hunter enters the cave
Then bids the wolves attack him in the enclave
Their work quickly done
Before the next sun
His mind sets the wolf free, no longer a slave

Once he could change victims into his kind
But that power is gone now, long left behind
What is a life worth
To wander the earth
Unable to die, on his own and maligned

IKO NAKAMURA

Iko Nakamura's from a village in Japan
He's seen far more than the average man
A hundred years old
His story now told
As I look for the secrets to long life spans

His village survives by the grace of the sea
Its bounty brought in by fishermen like he
The ocean is rough
But these men are tough
They set sail each day with no guarantee

The catch is shared equally with everyone
Whether only a pound or a metric ton
The gardens are tended
By families extended
Vegetables thrive in the hot summer sun

His seventh wife is young and slim
She cooks and cleans and cares for him
She lays him flat
On their tatami mat
And caters to his every whim

Many in the village are old and grey
But all say Iko is far and away
The oldest among
Those no longer young
And defer to him at the end of the day

I ask how he's managed to live so long
Whether exercise keeps his body strong
He shook his head
Then smiled and said,
"Those are the words but not the song."

"Eat fish and rice and Kirin beer
Tai Chi to cleanse both stress and fear
But the wisest sage
Always hides his age
I've been a hundred for over 20 years!"

IN DEMENTIA

Carl is a veteran of the second world war
He still gets around at age ninety-four
When things are misplaced
He searches in haste
But then he forgets what he's looking for

His dear wife Eileen is long passed away
He thinks of her often but not every day
When he can't recall
The woman on the wall
A sunny disposition suddenly turns grey

Some days are good and others not so
Why they turn bad he just doesn't know
So sits down and cries
Without knowing why
Staring at the ceiling or out the window

Sometimes he takes a long walk outside
To a coffee shop he went to with his bride
He orders two cups
To cheer himself up
And talks to Eileen who to him never died

Mary's the owner and old friend to Eileen
She knows the drill, it's a familiar scene
Pretending she's there
Mary speaks to the air
"It's so nice to see you, sugar or cream?"

Once a month veteran pals come around
They take him to the local VFW in town
Their uniforms pressed
And looking their best
War stories shared and sorrows drowned

Carl can't forget the German prison camp
The Winter of '41 was freezing and damp
Many soldiers died
Nazis warm inside
Their only heat came from the ceiling lamps

Back at home he forgets where he's been
But next month the guys will do it again
There's a benefit, too
Each time it seems new
These vets were once young badass men

Carl hasn't a car so can't drive to the store
For groceries he relies on Doris next door
She's made it quite plain
If he's Tarzan, she's Jane
But Eileen is gone and he'll love no more

Many years ago, Carl answered the call
And survived long enough to outlive 'em all
But the time comes to die
And as Carl says goodbye
Eileen looks on from a picture on the wall

INDIAN SUMMER

Finished hi school and had nothing planned
Hadn't been drafted for the war in Vietnam
Didn't know what to do
With opportunities few
Talked to my dad knowing he'd understand

He had this old Indian Chief in the yard
That back in the day he rode long and hard
It was gathering dust
So he said I must
Take it for the Summer on roads near and far

We cleaned it up nicely and fixed the ignition
Made us a seat 'cause the old one was missin'
Gaskets, a few
And it's good as new
That old motorcycle's in running condition

Filled up a knapsack with things I would need
For days on the road with my new trusty steed
Said 'bye to my dad
Who was both proud and sad
Recalling the times he lived for the speed

The first day soon ended and time for a rest
That ol' Indian Chief had passed its road test
A campground and fire
I'm ready to retire
Sausage with biscuits and hunger addressed

I traveled the Deep South where they say y'all
Cornbread and grits at the first rooster's call
Mardi Gras beads
Gumbo boil feeds
Back out on the road so my journey don't stall

Now Texas I found is at least two days wide
Cowgirls and Pearl beer help shorten the ride
New Mexican chilis
Cute senorita fillies
Then on to California without missing a stride

San Francisco hippies with flowers in their hair
Fisherman's Wharf and that cool Pacific air
Across the Golden Gate
To the Northwestern states
Snow-capped mountains, icy roads beware!"

The Great Plains stretch out as far as I can see
Wheat fields and dairy farms, feeling so free
I ride like the wind
My face a huge grin
Soon the Windy City with its high-rise panoply

On to the East and the Big Apple I travel
Tearing up blacktop, back roads and gravel
I check in with Dad
Both he and Mom sad
It seems that my plans are about to unravel

They tell me how sorry they couldn't afford
To send me to college and pay room and board
My draft notice came
But things aren't the same
For rich kids whose draft deferrals were scored

Nobody knows what tomorrow has in store
The Army might send me to the Vietnam war
But if I have to go
There's one thing I know
This country I've seen is worth fighting for

JENNY LEE

In the Spring of the year, I met Jenny Lee
A lovelier maiden there just couldn't be
Hair spun of gold
A look that foretold
This beauty could never see anything in me

I offered my hand though unsure if I should
She took it and said, "I was hoping you would!"
You don't get to dance
If you won't take a chance
An idea in the past I so misunderstood

The days ran to Summer and I was in love
Picnics on the meadow, the sun high above
This mysterious girl
Was the heart of my world
Still there were things she wouldn't speak of

We lay on the beach on a warm summer day
She says she must leave for a very short stay
It' just to attend
To a minor loose end
Returning before I even know she's away

Fall is upon us and the leaves start to turn
She's leaving more often but always returns
Frequently tired
Much sleep required
She says it's the weather, don't be concerned

Again she is gone but returns Christmas Eve
I confront her regarding the things I perceive
At last she reveals
What she's thus far concealed
An illness from which there can be no reprieve

We swear to each other we'll fight to the end
And continue through Winter as if life depends
But to no avail
The treatments have failed
We'll treasure what time the future may send

Arriving from work I will brew us some tea
She's snuggled by the fireside waiting for me
Her cheeks now gone cold
I don't have to be told
The cancer has taken my sweet Jenny Lee

JOB WITH A VIEW

Ivan arrived with his old country ways
And a fire in his heart that nothing could faze
Stepping off the boat
In a worn overcoat
With one suitcase that had seen better days

Ambition to spare but dollars so few
How to get started he hadn't a clue
So he signed a deal
To work the high steel
Skyscrapers rising; a job with a view

New York City in nineteen thirty-four
Buildings going up with ever more floors
Wrought iron's in demand
And Ivan's the man
To twist it and shape it into elevator doors

He'd been a blacksmith before he left home
Now wanted to open a shop of his own
So he worked up high
And put money by
Against the day he could get a small loan

Finally, Ivan could see his way clear
To leave the high steel and start a career
A shop with a phone
Became his new home
Small jobs at first to get out of arrears

His work was first-rate and soon Ivan found
He needed some help to hold backlog down
Hired a couple of men
And a few more then
His wrought iron became the talk of the town

His small shop grew into a huge factory
Well over a hundred well paid employees
Though work never slowed
He remained unbowed
Until something happened he couldn't foresee

A Union boss came to the job site one day
He gathered the workers and had this to say
"Just threaten to strike,
you'll get a pay hike,
and better benefits along with your pay."

The workers agreed so the man went to speak
With Ivan and told him he had just one week
To meet their demands
Or all to a man
Would walk out on strike with him up the creek

So the workers picketed outside the gate
Trucks couldn't come in to pick up their freight
And after a week
He came out to speak
Ivan told them they had sealed their own fate

The Foundry had bought the building and wares
Their greed had cost them but Ivan won't care
He'd thought them family
But now he could see
It always had been a one-sided affair

Money sufficient and troubles so few
A sad way to retire but what could he do?
Relaxed on the beach
Mai Tai within reach
He thinks, "Now, this is a job with a view!"

JULIE

Mister policeman I must speak with you
I'll tell you what I know to give you a clue
About a most chilling
Kidnap and killing
My name is Julie and I swear this is true

While we were sleeping my brother and me
Heard something coming and not quietly
We didn't know who
Might be coming through
'Cuz everything was dark and I couldn't see

My brother was struggling and softly crying
Then a gurgling sound as if he was trying
To catch a last breath
Before certain death
With that final gasp I knew he was dying

Just then a small ray of light filtered in
I saw something outside pulling at him
And then he was gone
Leaving me to stay on
That's when the light once again dimmed

Mother was hurt because I heard her scream
What have we done to make them so mean?
Will they come for me
And kill our family tree?
I hope things are not as bad as they seem

My little brother's gone although I can't see
I know he's no longer right here next to me
I miss him so much
His comforting touch
But I must remain until they set me free

If I were to die who would tell of our plight
Of all that happened to our family that night?
And what of our father
Did he even bother
To help us when he could have put up a fight?

So Mister policeman I've solemnly sworn
To help all I can even though I will mourn
The fate of my brother
And our loving mother
But you must wait a little while 'til I'm born

LADIES' NIGHT

There are 5 young women, the best of friends
Together since childhood and each depends
On the other four
Since first they swore
Their bond would forever not break or bend

Thru hi school and collage they stayed together
Found there's no storm the 5 cannot weather
All graduated
Then situated
Close to each other just like birds of a feather

They all are married and seek their own riches
But not in a way that makes others suspicious
In roundabout ways
Their secrecy pays
Did I mention that these 5 are actually witches?

These are modern day witches, stylish and chic
No bubbling cauldrons, tall hats or broomsticks
They cast secret spells
So no one can tell
The husbands are oblivious to their magic tricks

Once every month they meet at different sites
Informing their husbands, "It's Ladies Night!"
They're a pentagon
And when called upon
Can cast powerful spells at their monthly rites

A contract required signing but Joseph's client
In spite of his best efforts still remained silent
The 5 whispered then
"Client pick up the pen"
Joseph soon found him to be most compliant

Audrey's husband was in the foulest of moods
After golf on Sundays with his company's crew
They laugh at his game
And give him a name
Short Stroke Larry has to go home and stew

So Audrey sent him to a golf instructor friend
She's paid for some lessons so he must attend
Of course, there's a spell
But her husband can't tell
Larry wins the company tournament in the end

Laurie once cried at a meeting and confessed
She was newly pregnant and sorely distressed
Her man wants a boy
But he'll find no joy
"I carry a girl! Can this problem be addressed?"

The witches joined hands to form the pentagon
They brought forth a spell, "Give Laurie a son"
The months numbered nine
At the end of that time
Laurie birthed a boy and the casting was done

But trouble was brewing and witches can ken
Things of that nature and can often tell when
The 5 met that month
And each had a hunch
Something was troubling about one of their men

As the pentagon formed Miranda started crying
They all saw it too, there's no sense in denying
A terrible answer
The poor man has cancer
Why wouldn't her husband tell her he was dying?

A witch can move sickness from one to another
But Miranda couldn't cause someone to suffer
Her decision is made
It's she who will trade
But her husband will see her secret uncovered

When she returns home, she confesses to him
At first, he is shocked but knows what has been
He always believed
Nothing was achieved
Without her beside him thru thick and thru thin

She told him her plan, "Oh no!", he shuddered
"It's too late, my love", Miranda softly muttered
"I'm a witch, you see
and able to free
myself of the pain that you would have suffered."

LIVIN' DOLL

Millie was eight when her grandmother died
Along with her parents she sat by her side
The old lady smiled
Said, "Bless you, my child"
Her only granddaughter kissed her and smiled

Gramma said, "Emily, I've something for you."
And gave her a doll that was anything but new
"Please hold on to this
pretty little miss.
As long as she's with you, I'll be there, too."

In Gramma's day people made their own bread
Biscuits, cakes and pies kept a large family fed
No small paper packs
They bought flour in sacks
Made of printed cloth and quite large instead

She'd seen faded pictures of a Raggedy Ann
A doll people fashioned from a simple plan
And Gramma had picked
A flour sack fabric
From which to sew Annie with her own hand

After Gramma died Emily held the doll near
Soon Annie was speaking so Emily could hear
It was just in her head
As she lay in her bed
It was Gramma's soft voice so she didn't fear

Through Emily's school years Annie's advice
Helped her with her choices by thinking twice
Never led her astray
And graduation day
A job and apartment at a reasonable price

Emily succeeded at her job from the start
She enjoyed her work and took it to heart
Promotions a few
But all she could do
Was think about Danny when they were apart

They met in a coffee shop at lunch one day
Danny asked to join her and she said okay
Handsome and charming
A smile so disarming
Being close to him took her breath away

They dated for a year then Danny proposed
It seemed a good fit, her Annie supposed
"Let' give it a shot!"
So they tied the knot
But Emily's mother was silently opposed

Soon after the wedding her Danny got fired
For failing the drug tests that were required
Emily was thinking
He must have been drinking
A habit she knew he had recently acquired

Emily came home from her job every day
And cooked their supper in an effort to say
"It'll be all right"
But then late at night
Danny got drunk and moved further away

One day Danny was drunk out of his mind
He beat her so bad 'til her left eye was blind
She soothed it with ice
Then Annie's advice
"Go visit your mother but leave me behind."

She did as suggested in hopes of some peace
Her mother said she ought to call the police
But back in her flat
Annie didn't need that
She's determined to grant her Emily surcease

An anonymous call to 911 was contrived
The oven was on when the police arrived
There's no pilot light
The house is locked tight
Thanks to the booze Danny didn't survive

Now Danny was known to play with a knife
But the reason he wanted to find him a wife
Was he liked to eat
But avoided the heat
So Danny never, ever cooked a meal in his life

LOST TIME

Out in Blake County there's cattle and corn
One feeds the other as function feeds form
There are tractor pulls
And prize-winning bulls
Featured at the County Fair when it's warm

Farm animals brought in for the petting zoo
There's fried pork chops and corn dogs too
Canned fruit preserves
And if you've the nerve
Hit the corn maze and try to make it through

Nineteen seventy-five was a very good year
The corn grew tall with sweet yellow ears
The maze was prepared
In time for the fair
They made it so large you could disappear

On the very first day many kids went inside
Most were laughing but some of them cried
Then out walked a girl
With dimples and curls
Looking confused and with tears in her eyes

A nearby policeman asks her name and age
She's nine years old and named Carla Paige
And what's with the tears?
Her Mama's not here
Children often stray when Mom is engaged

He searches the grounds but finds little cheer
Locals only know of one Paige around here
Poor old Letty Paige
Has long been estranged
Ever since the day her daughter disappeared

With no other leads they take Carla around
To the one remaining Paige outside of town
When she opens the door
The old woman is floored
And clutches the folds of her dressing gown

How can this be, it's been thirty-seven years?
Mrs. Paige struggles to speak thru the tears
They'd gone to the fair
And while they were there
Carla went into the maze with her peers

After many days when she couldn't be found
Her father fell ill and dropped to the ground
He died the next day
And people would say
The loss of his daughter had taken him down

The black and white photo proves no mistake
A proud family of three and it shows the date
The nine-year old's there
Same dimples and hair
At the Blake County Fair nineteen thirty-eight

Carla will stay with her mother although
Old age will deny Mom the get-up-and-go
To keep up with the child
When she will run wild
But thankfully at last her baby's back home

Someone's little boy's been missing for days
Where he wandered off to no one can say
But one little girl
With dimples and curls
Thinks that he must have gone into the maze

Twenty twenty's here and it's been a long time
Letty Paige is long buried but Carla's just fine
After forty-five years
And millions of tears
The hurt that we carry is still here to remind

This year there won't be a Blake County Fair
No fried pork chops or memories to share
Thanks to Covid-19
It'll be a blank scene
The corn's tall and yellow but nobody cares

A farmer to carved a maze for us anyway
We've been sitting outside it now several days
Just like every year
We're waiting right here
For our lost little boy to walk out of the maze

MAGIC BEANS

Esther loved shopping on the internet
She's no shopaholic or even in debt
But a bargain for sure
Will hold some allure
Though she hasn't done anything foolish yet

One day while surfing she almost missed
A tiny little ad right there on Craig's List
Somebody it seems
Was selling some beans
The tiny ad was cute and it looked like this:

Something missing in your life?
Need a husband or a wife?
They're guaranteed
To fill your need
Get them at a special price

The odd thing was that there was no price
Just a telephone number and some advice
Please call for details
It's one of those sales
Where no advertisement will truly suffice

Curious she was and placed the phone call
Not sure what might happen, but after all
It's not every day
A deal comes your way
Though the odds that it's good are probably small

The lady who answered politely explained
There's only one way they may be obtained
If she wishes to buy
The seller requires
That she go there in person in order to claim

It's not very far and she's nothing to do
So agrees to the trip, why, wouldn't you?
With just a short drive
Esther has arrived
She's eager to learn the mysterious truth

The lady she meets is much older than her
Iced tea or coffee, which would she prefer?
The lady explains
"You must take great pains
to tell me your history so we may confer."

Esther revealed that her parents had died
In the camp at Auschwitz due to cyanide
When her last name is said
The old lady turns red
Crying the tears for so long never cried

"Your mother was my sister and I recall
how they took them away, once and for all.
We who were bakers,
chefs or shoemakers,
were spared the gas and the hanging wall."

Esther is dumbstruck and unable to speak
Hands are shaking and her knees are weak
Can't hold back the tears
After so many years
Or find the words she so desperately seeks

Her newfound aunt now talks of the beans
They don't exist but are merely a means
Of helping folks find
Others of their kind
Meant to be together as had been foreseen

No one really knows how it all got started
The one who began it is now long departed
But she knows the truth
Her aunt's name is Ruth
She's warm and caring and gentle-hearted

Ruth's husband found her in the same way
From a newspaper ad one bright sunny day
With no telephone
He came to her home
How he knew where he couldn't really say

Esther drives home and unpacks her things
Just as she's finishing the telephone rings
And so goes the plan
The caller's a man
"I'm calling about the Magic Beans . . . .

MEKONG RIVER WINE

Staff Sergeant Hart was in charge of supply
And nothing got past his meticulous eye
Not one paper clip
Ever gave him the slip
But Sarge was also an unscrupulous guy

The warehouse was an old water buffalo stall
His philosophy posted up high on the wall
In here I am King
If you need anything
You'll take it my way or not get it at all

Mekong River Wine was a local rice liquor
It made you sick and then made you sicker
But once you got used
To the abdominal abuse
It got you quite drunk ever quicker and quicker

The Black Market thrived in Vietnam back then
And Hart was the most opportunistic of men
The market was there
And he wanted his share
But how to get product from suppliers to them?

Pay Certificates is how we were paid
But the Vietnamese wouldn't take them in trade
Those who'd just joined
Still had US coin
So he bought the new dollars at a generous rate

Then he bought whiskey and marked it up high
Selling all he could get to Marines and G.I,'s
It went round and round
Getting booze from the town
Trading Certificates for dollars to buy

Sarge was getting rich but a problem arose
After each bit of trading a question was posed
He had no real money
Now isn't that funny?
Those certificates can't be readily disposed

If he waited until he went back to the states
And tried to cash out with that much weight
Red flags would be raised
It would all go sideways
They'd be confiscated and jail would await

After much consideration he arrived at a plan
The Exchange had many costly items on hand
Nikon cameras, a few
Bulova wristwatches too
He'd ship them back home to resell when he can

Every dollar he made was sent home in this way
His wife would take care of it until came the day
His twenty was in
And that would be when
They'd retire to an island to feel the ocean spray

The time finally came and he headed back home
Anxiously wondering how his nest egg had grown
But his house had been sold
And the new owners told
To hand him a letter, her whereabouts unknown

She wrote that investigators came to the door
Looking for the things he had asked her to store
But she'd been ahead
And sold it all instead
Now she was waiting at an island seashore

MEMORY GARDENS

Barely eighteen and he's just killed a man
They lie close together in the tropical sand
He'll kill many more
But never keep score
He silently curses this war with Japan

The enemy he's killed is no older than he
His buttons are open and inside he sees
A small oilskin packet
Tucked in his jacket
He'll carry it with him as a memento mori

The Pacific war rages but it's finally won
By exacting surrender from the Rising Sun
Those who survive
Many barely alive
Can never forget the things they have done

He never got married and couldn't say why
Kept mostly to himself as time scurried by
For some it's OK
But soon comes the day
We ask if we've made the most of our lives

The images in the pouch are always in mind
He wonders if she would be possible to find
A town square is shown
So perhaps it is known
To one who could help and be so inclined

After a long journey a man has been found
Who knows of the woman and of the town
She's in a tea garden
And so to beg pardon
He bows at her table and asks to sit down

She silently nods to this curious man
Who opens a pouch he has in his hand
An audible sigh
When she looks inside
The flood of old memories unable to stand

Some things are known without being said
Who but his killer would so honor the dead?
But she doesn't feel hate
For the man who's come late
He too fought in the war and surely has bled

All over Japan Memory Gardens exist
As the hauntings of war are wont to persist
A brief respite needed
So an hour conceded
Refreshes the spirit while there in its midst

They sit hand in hand in a flowery glen
No more need be said by her or by him
A whimper is heard
But does not disturb
As she cries for her loss and he for his sin

MISSIN' YOU

Staring in the mirror at a three-day stubble
I oughta shave but it's too much trouble
I've got lots to do
Like missin' you
So I'll start by pouring myself a double

I remember a time when my best friend
Was a gal who promised me 'til the end
Now down on my luck
They took back my truck
You and the bank have left me to fend

Working a farm isn't meant for just one
Chores never end in the hot baking sun
Fields to be plowed
With no rest allowed
Put up and feed the mule when I'm done

It's been a long time since you went away
If you're now happy then I guess it's OK
I'll struggle along
Though you done me wrong
But I'm missin' you at the end of each day

Our old well ran dry so a new one was dug
Didn't know how to pay so I took to my jug
But while they were digging
A collapse in the rigging
As oil started gushing and they had to plug

No one believed Oklahoma had crude
This far to the West but interest's renewed
Crops don't need growing
With oil always flowing
I've got a new truck but the same attitude

Now I am saddled with legal paperwork
I don't understand so I hired me a clerk
A lawyer to explain
Why I'm signing my name
I hate this new stuff but I do like the perks

The dogs are all happy and the mule is too
I should share in their joy in all that is new
But they cannot see
It's just not in me
'Cause in spite of it all I'm still missin' you

Seems everyone now has something to sell
Even long-lost cousins are ringing my bell
But it's no surprise
Like horses draw flies
My money's attracting the family from hell

Now you are back after all of these days
Cryin' and beggin' to come home and stay
I'm sorry, my dear
You've no future here
Missin' you's better than sufferin' your ways

MY BACK PORCH

I wait for the morning sun to burn off the mist
Gazing at the flowers the night dew has kissed
The bees' buzzing sound
Fills the air all around
The smell of fresh coffee impossible to resist

Days are now longer since summer is here
The animals seem to like this time of year
The earth is in bloom
And each one makes room
'Cause this is the time for new life to appear

This morning the bird bath is a popular site
Robins and sparrows are preparing for flight
It's beautiful weather
As they wash their feathers
Nestlings must be fed before comes the night

My backyard is home to a hummingbird feeder
Sweet syrup hangs from the branch of a cedar
The little ones hover
Beneath its lush cover
And jockey for position with me as cheerleader

The wild rabbits eat all the vegetables I grow
I haven't got the heart to hurt them and so
The flowers are fine
But the veggies aren't mine
I raise them so Bugs leaves the daffodils alone

I've got brown squirrels living in my trees
Not scared of me they're as bold as you please
One sits on the rail
Leans back on his tail
And eats what he's found, not sharing with me

A doe and her fawn have just come into view
Two beautiful creatures right out of the blue
They graze without fear
A buck must be near
Maybe some corn will say, "You're welcome, too!"

I've found my own place in the country air
Much slower than the hectic rat race out there
No telephones here
To ring and interfere
With my reverie as I sit in my back porch chair

MY CABIN

Built a log cabin near a juniper stand
A suitable size for an unmarried man
It has a big tub
Which I sit in and scrub
The dirt I accumulate working the land

Make my own whiskey so needed a well
Dug it myself for my moonshine to sell
My cornstalks are tall
When I harvest in Fall
Light up the still and sit back for a spell

My life on the hill
Is all I have known
With only my still
I feel so alone

Met a young lady at a local barn dance
She seemed really nice so I took a chance
Showed her the home
I raised up alone
Built by my hand with no need to finance

I've masculine things like bear rugs and such
Said what it needed was a soft woman's touch
I'm not fond of change
But she began to arrange
My life in a way that I didn't like much

I'm set in my ways
And best left alone
I've found that it pays
To care for my own

Soon we had curtains and lace all around
Outside were flowers disguising the ground
Porcelain dishware
"Wipe your feet, have a care!"
Man, how I hated that shrill piercing sound

Then came the cross that couldn't be borne
The still and the moonshine had to be gone
Said liquor's a sin
And that did her in
They never will find her there under the corn

MY GMC

I work in a sawmill six days of the week
Sundays are for fishing at Miller's Creek
I saved up my pay
Lookin' to the day
I'd get a new truck as mine's an antique

It took a long time but I could finally see
My way clear to purchase that big GMC
So I drove it away
On that glorious day
My long-held dream was at last a reality

The biggest diesel engine money can buy
Goin' down the highway the miles seem to fly
Got cruise control
And a center console
That keeps a tall boy cold while you drive

Heated, reclining, massaging bucket seats
Rolled up and tucked with two-tone pleats
Pads for the shoulders
Heated cup holders
Tufted floor mats where you put your feet

That first Saturday night I headed to town
Intending to do a little foolin' around
Have some innocent fun
Maybe meet someone
Listen to some music with a country sound

I bragged on my truck to a cute little gal
Next thing I know she's got me corralled
Wound up in my bunk
And she didn't seem drunk
Quite a night it was on the high chapparal

Rolled out in the mornin' like a broncin' buck
Thanking my stars for this one stroke of luck
Hoped I didn't blow it
But wouldn'tcha know it
The thieving little hussy ran off with my truck

MY PROSTATE

Women often say men don't have a clue
We can't understand the things they go through
I'm sure that's the truth
I know back in my youth
Each month the mood changes baffled anew

But as we grow older our bodies must change
Hormones with age make cells rearrange
And that is the cause
For her menopause
But men don't escape it completely unscathed

That damn little prostate has plans of its own
To show how it hates me now that it's grown
My bladder is squeezed
As tight as you please
Six trips to the toilet and a night's sleep is blown

She's now the one who can't understand
My lack of excitement for what she had planned
My amorous side
Is nearing ebb tide
Thanks to the efforts of that sinister gland

NEIGHBORS

Harold has a Chris Craft he takes out fishin'
George lives next door but he's only wishin'
'Cuz he can't afford
A boat to fish aboard
So pissin' off Harold is his new life's ambition

George has a Doberman that poops a lot
Feeds him a diet that really makes him squat
At his encouragement
The dog leaves excrement
Under Harold's boat where it's so hard to spot

But Harold's no fool and doesn't want a fight
He invites George out fishin' to George's delight
They return home early
With George mad and surly
He's burnt to a crisp and never got a bite

George treats his sunburn with lots of cold beer
His wife says, "It isn't Harold's fault, dear."
But he doesn't listen
And swears off of fishin'
He's plotting his revenge with a maniacal sneer

He wanders next door with a large butcher knife
Stands in the foyer and threatens Harold's life
Harold laughs in his face
Calls him a disgrace
"The joke is on you, I'm sleeping with your wife!"

George's wife sneaks up behind her crazed man
She's holding her biggest cast iron frying pan
Hits George in the head
And knocks him stone dead
So what do they do with a body on their hands?

Harold's wife returns from shopping at the store
Before they can move George's body on the floor
She sees them embrace
Spots the fear on his face
The suspicions she's had are proven and more

She reaches for the gun she's got for protection
And stares at her husband with zero affection
Shoots him five times
Relishing her crime
George's wife looks on but raises no objection

Both bodies are loaded in the boat after dark
Then driven down to the boat launching park
They wait patiently
Until night falls at sea
To scuttle the boat and swim past the sharks

They make their way home without detection
Using dark streets and alleys for protection
At home in dry clothes
And nobody knows
We've handled things quietly and to perfection

Next day the police are notified they're missin'
Two husbands who yesterday went out fishin'
The car isn't here
And they took lots of beer
"We told them don't go but they didn't listen."

Evenings at dusk the neighbors meet outside
The Doberman sleeping on the patio beside
The insurance has paid
And they both have it made
So sip their wine coolers and chortle with pride

NEW KID

He doesn't recall what his father was like
Being so young when the man took a hike
His Mom does her best
Works all day without rest
Still she could never afford that new bike

He tells her, "Don't worry, everything is OK."
Yet wonders why his life is going this way
As they move around
From town to strange town
In each place he hopes they can finally stay

He's always the new kid in every school
Learning the ropes and a new set of rules
He earns B's and C's
Tries his hardest to please
But teenagers can be so unwittingly cruel

Life has its ups and its downs that's for sure
Some folks are rich but so many are poor
Lunch in a bag
Jeans turning to rags
How much more can a young man endure?

In the past he has tried to relate what he fears
The terrible hatred he feels for his peers
Wherever he's been
He never fit in
His pleas for understanding fall on deaf ears

His mother thinks he's just going thru a phase
Teachers believe he is starving for praise
He uses free time
Engaging in crime
Police warn him that he must change his ways

If no one can hear you then raise up your voice
Make it so loud that you leave them no choice
Tell them that you
Are a real person too
You only ever wanted to be one of the boys

So he steals someone's gun and lays out a plan
The school is his target and those he can't stand
In a frenzy of killing
He screams out a chilling
"Now that you hear me, can you understand?"

NIGHTMARES

Kids see monsters whenever they're scared
"Look in my closet, it's hiding in there!"
Or under their bed
Waiting to be fed
They are what give little children nightmares

Such a frightened child was Jenny Olstead
In the middle of the night she'd crawl into bed
With her mom and dad
Because she was scared
The monster in her room fills her with dread

Night after night she's afraid to go to sleep
The closet would open and out it would creep
Then one night she stayed
Perhaps unafraid?
So Mom and Dad slept never hearing a peep

So proud of her brave little Jenny Mom made
Her favorite breakfast, toast and marmalade
But Jenny slept late
And at quarter to eight
She went to wake her so she wouldn't be late

Bloody pajamas are strewn across the floor
And a wet red trail leads to the closet door
But nothing's in there
Except for thin air
Mom calls out to her but Jenny's no more

The families are always suspected at first
Their stories may sound a little rehearsed
But who would believe
That they could conceive
Of killing their child which is surely the worst?

The police search the house but to no avail
There's no forced entry and no outside trail
No conclusion is drawn
The girl is just gone
Months with no leads so the case goes stale

Then the Olmstead's sold out and moved away
They couldn't bear to stay another day
A young family bought
The house they had sought
One they would like at a price they could pay

Their young son now had a room of his own
A place he could live until he's full grown
But the very first night
He dropped out of sight
The same blood trail but not a hair or a bone

Detectives recalled the Jenny Olstead case
Similarities are staring us straight in the face
The house is the same
But what is to blame?
We never solved it so we're in the same place

The investigation is once again stalled
Kids' bloody clothing is laying there sprawled
But the child's disappeared
As the police had feared
Media blames the cops for dropping the ball

Just as before the parents chose to leave
They must get away in order to grieve
The house will not sell
Someone always tells
Prospective buyers not to be deceived

Drug users sometimes go there to get high
If one should go missing police will drop by
The same bloody clothes
And that's how it goes
They're left without a body to identify

NOT THIS CHILD

A young wife named Pari longed for a child
Her husband Aditya goes the extra mile
Yet no pregnancy's occurred
No life within her stirred
So Aditya concludes he must be infertile

To console his wife Aditya visits his friend
Arjun is someone on whom he can depend
He offers advice
That comes with a price
Yet there is a way that may work in the end

Arjun suggests he could father their son
If it remains secret the deed they have done
It can't be unhidden
For this is forbidden
Aditya's family would be publicly shunned

And so it was done in the dark of the night
All of them swearing to keep their lips tight
And wait to be told
It had taken hold
That which would foster the ultimate delight

Finally young Pari began to gain girth
And soon the time came for her to give birth
The midwife sent word
A cry could be heard
And Aditya was the happiest man on earth

But in their room Pari was deep in despair
Never believing life could be so unfair
Giving birth to a girl
Had shattered her world
"Let him still love me", a whispered prayer

"Arjun betrayed us!", Pari screams aloud
"What of the fields that have to be plowed?"
Aditya must demand
Arjun's son work their land
She says Arjun failed to do what he vowed

Aditya faces Arjun with this wild accusation
Arjun does his best to calm his frustration
No man can decide
What his seed will provide
Aditya is responsible for his own situation

Chastised and embarrassed Aditya returns
Relates how his protestations were spurned
Too late now to blame
But have you a name?
Pari's chosen Anika, as Aditya soon learns

Now age eighteen Anika's beauty is known
To all and the men of the village have shown
A keen admiration
Through shameless flirtation
But Sanjit holds her heart, he and he alone

Now Arjun seeks the girl for his youngest son
And with this exclamation Aditya is stunned
"She'll marry Vijay
or I'll tell of the day
I fathered that girl and she'll marry no one!"

Aditya and Pari are now forced to confess
To Anika the events that led up to this mess
But to marry her brother
Neither Father nor Mother
Can ask their lovely daughter to acquiesce

Anika has arranged to meet Sanjit that day
As her parents grieve she silently slips away
When Sanjit hears her story
He tells her not to worry
In soft whispered words she had this to say:

"The truth of my nature gives lie to my worth.
I'll spare my family the shame of my birth."
The last words they'll say
On their final day,
"We'll marry in heaven if not here on earth."

PAROLE DATE

Edgar Cawley had been eagerly sought
But killed 4 women before he was caught
Throughout his brief trial
He just sat and smiled
His lawyer's arguments all came to naught

The state didn't have the death penalty
If they couldn't kill him he'd never be free
A hundred-year bit
For each vicious hit
And the four were to run consecutively

When he was asked if he'd anything to say
Edgar replied, "I'll be paroled one day."
He seemed to believe
There'd be a reprieve
The judge just said, "Take this man away!"

Everyone laughed at the thought of parole
He'd have to live to four hundred years old
Even good behavior
Wouldn't be his savior
This guy will die in some stinking rat hole

Like all headline stories Edgar's would die
Age fades them away without even a sigh
Left to turn rotten
Edgar's forgotten
And time slips away in the blink of an eye

Fifty years on and the prison's unchanged
Neither is Edgar 'cuz he's just as deranged
He seems the same mostly
But if one looks closely
He's not aged a day in spite of the chains

A hundred years pass then a hundred more
Edgar knows exactly 'cuz he keeps score
All over his wall
Little tick marks crawl
When they hit 350 he'll bang on the door.

Wardens in the prison come and they go
A new one takes over and wants to know
By his arrival date
How this one inmate
Could have come here so many years ago

The guards are puzzled and can't explain
No one here notices day to day change
When old guards retire
Replacements are hired
They don't introduce the prisoners by name

How was old Edgar able to live so long?
A deal with the devil gone horribly wrong?
Even if it's true
He's nowhere near due
For early release so let's just get along

The day arrives when Edgar can apply
For early release since he hasn't died
The parole board looks
At the prison books
And sees that it must allow Edgar outside

Much has changed in the intervening years
Prison is outdated but the public's fear
Has caused them to hold
Until their parole
Remaining inmates 'til the prison is cleared.

So Edgar's released into a world unknown
He thinks he must be in the Twilight Zone
Moving sidewalks
Taxicabs that talk
And the worst part of all, Edgar's all alone

Suddenly everything turns completely black
Sharp aching pain and his body goes slack
When he awakens
He sees he's been taken
To a dark room where he is flat on his back

He seems to be lying in some kind of box
All along the sides it's configured with locks
He's strapped in it tight
And in the dim light
He sees a man opening a large toolbox

"My name is Sam Austin but you don't know
the names of your victims nor do you show
any remorse
when you are the source
of their pain when you strike the fatal blow."

"I made the same deal as you way back then.
Even though I couldn't know where or when
I'd catch up to you
but I certainly knew
I'd have my revenge when I saw you again."

"You killed my wife in a murderous rage.
Now I have got you locked up in a cage.
I know you won't die
up there in the sky
but oh my, what a war your mind will wage."

"In this time the world is so populated
the custom of burial has become outdated.
There's a huge space station
used for inhumation
where coffins like this are concentrated."

Sam closes the lid and locks it down tight
It's placed in line for the next space flight
No one will lament
A killer who went
Still kicking and screaming into eternal night

I wonder which one paid the greatest cost
The one who must live with a terrible loss
Or the murderous thug
So incredibly smug
That he whispered to fate, "I am the boss!"

PENNY MAE

Dreams are but yarns we spin in our sleep
From our subconscious they silently creep
Some are amusing
Others confusing
A few contain secrets we struggle to keep

Then there are those that leave us terrified
With butterflies of fear still fluttering inside
Though we awaken
Still, we are shaken
Not even the sunlight can make it subside

Such was a dream that came to Penny Mae
Returning every night and haunting her day
Behind every door
Poor Penny was sure
The thing that pursued her there silently lay

Her dream changed a bit each passing night
The danger got closer but still out of sight
Penny could feel it
Though' darkness concealed it
She felt it was evil but how could she fight?

The swampland at night is a dangerous place
Where one can disappear and leave no trace
It's there Penny finds
From deep in her mind
Her struggle plays out in a most deadly race

The harder she tries the less progress is made
Her feet are mired down, so heavily weighed
With each step she sinks
And tries hard to think
Then suddenly wakes up shaking and afraid

She tells her best friend about her nightmare
Anna sympathizes and assures her she cares
Hugs her friend tight
And says, "It's all right!"
But Penny's uncertain and whispers a prayer

How many more nights 'til she can't get away?
She tries to stay awake but can only delay
This time is the last
The blackness moves fast
Now her feet are trapped and she is just prey

Her eyes are wide open and her mouth is too
Fingers clutch the sheets so hard they are blue
Her body is sprawled
As if she had crawled
But whatever killed Penny hasn't left any clues

Anna is astonished to learn that Penny's died
Her nightmare must have pushed her to suicide
But life must go on
And before the next dawn
Anna dreams of a swamp and an evil it hides

PLACEBO

Five Star Pharma has received permission
To test a new drug that may cause remission
In patients with cancer
Seeking an answer
Is there any treatment for their condition?

A double-blind regimen is how it will go
Integrity vital so no one may know
Which patient receives
The drug they believe
May help them and who gets the placebo

One lab prepares the drug to be tested
Another supplies the placebos requested
Which one goes to whom
No one can assume
Safeguarding the data must be uncontested

Dave is a researcher whose brilliant ideas
Have been overlooked since he's been working here
But this round of tests
Will see Dave at his best
He's making placebos or so it appears

Dave has developed a cure for this disease
Substituting the placebo should be a breeze
He wants to make sure
They know there's a cure
Such an opportunity is one he must seize

The trial is over and unbelievably
Half of the subjects are now cancer free
A miracle to some
In the lab there is one
Whose vindication has arrived finally

Dave is called in to explain what he's done
He freely admits that his drug is the one
That was given to those
Scheduled for placebos
In an effort to finally put cancer on the run

Dave's now unemployed and was never paid
Results of the testing have been hidden away
Patient interviews declined
Non disclosures were signed
Treatment, not cures, is where the money is made

POOR HENRY

Henry shuffles through the dark alleyway
His seedy clothes are tattered and frayed
To protect his feet
From the cold, wet street
Cardboard shoes he must change every day

Sometimes the shelter might offer him a bed
If he arrives early but who plans ahead?
He sleeps where the rats
Fight people for scraps
In his once wavy hair new head lice are bred

The country club lifestyle was left far behind
Cocaine and booze raised hell with his mind
When he hit the skids
His wife took the kids
Away to a place she hopes he'll never find

His friends felt sorry but what can you do?
Poor Henry fell prey to the blow and the brew
But a cocaine drought
When the money ran out
Left him a quivering wreck through and through

He has no acquaintances but for Maureen
Whom others call the Shopping Cart Queen
She shows him the ropes
And openly hopes
Poor Henry survives the bad she has seen

Maureen has told him of the vampire deaths
Whether their habits were cocaine or meth
They each met their end
Sans family or friend
Their blood was taken with their last breaths

There were two little holes in the jugular vein
Red swollen skin around tiny bloodstains
To one always high
It was a vampire
A rational explanation to a muddled brain

Although in withdrawal Henry still had his wits
So had no patience for such crazy bullshit
He's suffering still
With fever and chills
And his mind's occupied with vomiting fits

Along comes a man called Back Alley John
Who wants to help Henry bounce back strong
John sympathizes
And empathizes
This is the same thing that he's undergone

"I've seen everything that you're going through.
Money's all gone and friends deserted you.
You've got the DT's,
you're down on your knees.
But your life has value, I swear that it's true."

Henry improves under John's ministrations
'Til Maureen finds the jugular penetrations
As white as a sheet
Far back from the street
Life drained from his body, exsanguination

In spite of the depths to which poor Henry sank
His recent recovery left one man to thank
Ol' Back Alley John
Whom he relied on
A valued employee of the Midtown Blood Bank

PRISON BLUES

For thirty-six years I was stuck in that hole
On 5 counts of murder, no chance of parole
The bulls aren't kind
They're all of one mind
Driving us mad was their ultimate goal

Something that all of them don't understand
Is in none of those killings did I have a hand
My one alibi
Instead chose to lie
I wonder if getting me blamed was his plan

My wife thought I did it so she got a divorce
The kids came to visit but talking was forced
As they slowly grew
We all of us knew
The meetings would end with a bit of remorse

The police came to see me about the old crime
They'd something to say after all of that time
With a new kind of screen
The blood at the scene
Had been proven at last that it never was mine

A fistful of business cards strewn on my cot
Lawyers who'll sue for the raw deal I got
What they talked about
Was that when I got out
The state would pay big time for letting me rot

I walked down the streets of a city so changed
People and places unfamiliar and strange
The money received
For a life so aggrieved
Cannot for a small piece of mind be exchanged

Although I am free there are many who grieve
Some stood in court to oppose my reprieve
They threaten and yell
They'll send me to hell
And nothing will stop them I truly believe

Now on the run I can't stop or slow down
I had to put miles between me and that town
As I grow older
Looking over my shoulder
I wish I was back on that bleak prison ground

PRISON BREAK

When one is handed life without parole
Nothing to lose makes one lose control
The thought of escape
Begins to take shape
No turning back once the idea takes hold

Charlie Kirk had always gotten out before
He could fool any lock and open any door
So they sent him to
A place called 'The Zoo'
Confident he wouldn't escape any more

Built far from the city on the desert sand
Escaping The Zoo was already planned
The hot burning sun
With nowhere to run
Will soon land the prisoner back in hand

After several months of playing the scout
Charlie feels sure he's found a way out
He's going AWOL
Down under the wall
By digging a tunnel with a concave route

He dug all night and put the dirt in his pants
Left it in the yard when he got the chance
The wind was the tide
That spread it out wide
So no one would notice with a casual glance

In just a few months the tunnel was complete
Charlie crawled through and rose to his feet
As he looks around
There isn't a sound
Something is wrong but he will not retreat

There's tropical jungle as far as he can see
In the middle of the desert how can this be?
There are fruit bearing trees
And a soft wafting breeze
A pond of water and a spring that runs free

However far he travels in any direction
He always ends up in the same small section
In circles, it seems
As if in a dream
Every escape attempt is met with deception

The sun never sets and the rain doesn't fall
Yet plants still bear fruit and grow ever tall
The Garden sans Eve
No chance of reprieve
Alone in a place where the birds never call

There's plenty of food and he's water to drink
It's better than prison, or so you might think
But with no living soul
Around to console
Charlie now knows just how far one can sink

PROM NIGHT

It was nearing the time for graduation
The class was filled with anticipation
But the Senior Prom
Would just be a bomb
For two in the class there'll be no carnation

Charlie Timmons was the senior class nerd
Chess Club president whose vision's blurred
Wore horn-rimmed glasses
Aced all his classes
But a date for the Prom was downright absurd

Then there's Julie Langford, a shy little girl
With eyes slightly crossed and tumbling curls
She has Downs Syndrome
And must stay at home
The Prom will be held in a different world

But Mister Timmons held a different view
And told his son Charlie what he should do
"Why don't you ask Jools?"
(They were friends at school)
"You'd make a great couple, the two of you."

So Julie and Charlie decided to go
Their parents were pleased and told them so
The others may sneer,
"What are they doing here?"
But it's their Prom, too, so on with the show

Charlie's dad drives them, as proud as can be
Their limo is his beat up Jeep Cherokee
But nothing can dim
The mood they're all in
It's the first date for both and they're jittery

When they arrive the sniggering begins
Whispered voices wonder how they got in
Giggles and laughter
Ensued thereafter
But Charlie and Jools each had a tough skin

The band for the prom was a local one
And Charlie is friends with the leader's son
They've known each other
For years, like brothers
And jammed with the band on some dry runs

Charlie's a maestro when holding a guitar
Once had a dream he'd become a rock star
And Julie could sing
A voice that could bring
Any house down but she'd never get that far

Late in the evening the leader of the band
Asked the audience to give a big hand
For two of their own
Who so far unknown
Might someday be famous throughout the land

Charlie and Julie made their way to the stage
They did pop ten numbers and became the rage
The students rejoiced
At guitar and voice
These two were so talented for kids of their age

But while they were playing a scream is heard
A boy on the dance floor's dying is the word
So Julie jumps down
In her evening gown
Something familiar within her has stirred

Many bad things can accompany Downs
Epilepsy, for one, as Julie had found
She studied them all
If one came to call
Better to be ready than die on the ground

The boy on the floor's in an epileptic fit
If he swallows his tongue, that's the end of it
A barrette from her hair
With no time to spare
Is pushed through his tongue in a bloody split

Julie tells the others to hold the boy down
Let the seizure pass, never mind the sounds
The boy recovered
And all the others
Applauded Julie Langford, forgetting her Downs

RADIO FLYER

I remember the Christmas when I was nine
Lights on the tree made it sparkle and shine
A fine sight to see
The tag said to me
That Radio Flyer I'd been wanting was mine

I soon grew tired of pulling my sister around
A genuine purpose would have to be found
Still shiny and new
It needs something to do
But not much happening in our small town

Mom says she needs to buy groceries today
With so much to do she just can't get away
She gives me a list
Asks, "Can you fill this
if I call ahead so you won't have to pay?"

To the grocer I went with my wagon in tow
Neighbor kids jealous as they watched me go
My wagon was full
But no effort to pull
All the way home with my precious cargo

Soon I went shopping every Saturday
And once a lady stopped me on the way
She asked, "Please could you
shop for me, too?"
"I've been so sick lately and I'll gladly pay."

I did as she asked and made a quarter tip
My Radio Flyer was now a merchant ship
Told Mom she was ill
And instead of a pill
Took her a home cooked meal my next trip

Word got around about my Mom's cooking
People asked me if she accepted bookings
I sold my mom's meals
On that wagon's wheels
Often you'll find when you aren't looking

After a while Mom grew tired of the toil
I decided to invest my share of the spoils
Bought a push mower
From its previous owner
Pulled on my wagon with gas can and oil

I mowed lawns until I finished high school
Left my baby brother the wagon and tools
And I took with me
Life lessons learned free
Hard work instills a respect for life's rules

Now kids have iPads and smart telephones
Texting each other at school and at home
A Radio Flyer
Was my one desire
And I miss it today although I'm full grown

RED CROSS KIDS

Big city streets provide little room for play
But kids are resourceful and soon find a way
This group however
Was even more clever
As a girl in the group faced hardship one day

Her family was evicted for not making the rent
Little as it was for their shabby tenement
Out on the street
A harsh fate to meet
Her Dad killed in war and now this sad event

A basement unused would suffice for a while
Not a big change from their previous lifestyle
Tommy's parents know
But for grace there we go
Welcome them as they endure this new trial

They vow to rely on their own neighborhood
Believing that people are basically good
Food still in cans
To provide helping hands
Blankets and toiletries, "Please, if you could!"

Response is tremendous and plenty of stuff
Is piled in the basement but it's not enough
If this works for one
We're surely not done
Many must find that the going is tough

At last the girl's Mother has found work to do
Earning enough so that they can start anew
While Mom is away
She decides to repay
By joining the cause that saw them all through

Red Cross Kids is the name they have taken
Their motto, "Let no family ever be forsaken!"
Until graduation
Train the next generation
Go into the world and bring home the bacon

Their efforts move forward and many are spared
Times of desperation 'cause they are prepared
A canned food buffet
And warm place to stay
But the best gift of all is that somebody cared

These pioneers now have kids of their own
Their time as Red Cross Kids clearly has shown
Success isn't measured
In money and treasure
Giving to others is the triumph they've known

Regardless of the state of the 'Me Generation'
You'll find in the cities across this great nation
Youngsters who've learned
Satisfaction is earned
Helping their neighbors in times of privation

REQUIEM FOR A CITY

This is the city I used to know well
But what you see now is merely a shell
The heart of it's gone
But the folks must stay on
If no one is buying then how can you sell?

Ms. Carter on the corner would see me and wave
And speak of the husband she knew to be brave
He was killed in Iraq
By a roadside attack
The medics worked hard but just couldn't save

Factory buildings are closed and rust-stained
The jobs move away but the workers remained
Now unemployed
They couldn't avoid
The greed of big business today unrestrained

This little bodega's been robbed many times
Thieves never got more than nickels and dimes
The judge sets 'em free
To continue their spree
But shoplifting beer is the least of their crimes

The park where the kids used to go to play ball
Was lost to make way for a new shopping mall
The plans though fell through
And so the weeds grew
Now it's a dumping ground garbage and all

Drugs are the new way of life around here
With them come violence, anger and fear
Gangs must compete
For control of the street
Children learn early of whom to steer clear

The hospital tries to continue to serve
But most paramedics are losing their nerve
With ambulance runs
Under fire from guns
Danger awaits them around every curve

I was a policeman and this was the beat
I walked every day though it blistered my feet
But drugs can't be sold
With a cop on patrol
So I was murdered, gunned down in the street

RIVERBOAT GAMBLER

The Mississippi River hosts many a boat
But the Natchez Queen is the finest afloat
Two hundred feet long
And fabled in song
She's simply 'The Queen', as the poet wrote

Her gambling hall is as posh as the Ritz
Filled with the trappings of glamour and glitz
Candle chandeliers
Gold inlaid mirrors
Upholstered armchairs where the players sit

Cole Delancy is a gambler who preys
On folks who live along The Queen's way
At each stop they board
When they can afford
A game that's illegal in their town to play

He keeps a derringer strapped to his ankle
In case a poor loser gets overly rankled
So far just the sight
Of it's ended the fight
A fact for which Cole is sincerely thankful

Lily Rountree worked in mining town saloons
During the 1800's gold mining boom
When the gold played out
She wandered about
And met up with Cole in a smoky card room

She took to Cole the first time she laid eyes
They devised a con game to work as allies
As Lily served drinks
Her long lashes winked
Broadcasting to Cole cards held by the guys

Aboard The Queen it worked to perfection
But shills were required to avoid detection
In each town they found
A man who was down
And let him win to conceal his connection

When folks who knew him saw that he won
It didn't seem likely there might be a con
But a man named Slade
Had already made
The connection and knew whom to lean upon

He cornered Lily next night at the bar
As a West coast gambler, he'd traveled far
If she joined with him
Together they'd win
Then head to 'Frisco where she'd be a star

So at the next game Slade started winning
Cole figured it out right from the beginning
His nod to the shill
To go for the kill
Would leave them both happily grinning

Law on the river's not the same as in town
No city constable or policemen around
You do what is right
Or be ready to fight
Treat a man wrong and he'll take you down

Slade wasn't told and the shill was denied
So he told the table how the two conspired
Lily broke her oath
So Cole shot them both
The players all agreed it was justified

SAFETY NET

Unbidden it arrives from the darkness of space
Its mission to obliterate the entire human race
Preparing the way
For the coming day
When others of its kind will arrive to replace

The ones who came first know this enemy well
It roams through the cosmos inflicting its hell
Inhabitants excised
Their world colonized
Then on to the next when its numbers swell

But it's come at a time of miraculous events
When the people of the desert still live in tents
Sand being shifted
Enormous weights lifted
Structures are erected that make little sense

Great pyramids built from huge blocks of stone
Intended as the Pharaoh's eternal throne
Their locations are
Aligned with the stars
But for reasons privy to the architects alone

Obelisks arise in many selected locations
Forming a grid of interconnected stations
A planetary maze
Laid out in arrays
So one always points at the desired destination

Work is not finished when the demon arrives
So a battle ensues high above in the skies
Now petroglyphs show
The scenes blow by blow
When the enemy was driven to a fiery demise

It took many years to complete the construction
Today many pyramids are local reproductions
But ancient Egypt was
The beginning because
Geographically it offered the fewest obstructions

The work was completed and time to move on
So these benevolent beings were finally gone
After thousands of years
It's now becoming clear
There just might be a conclusion to be drawn

Could it be that a worldwide network's control
Rests in the pyramids, not the Pharaoh's soul?
If the demon returns
Will the Earth burn?
Or can a signal to Orion send it back to its hole?

Many have asked whether we are alone
If they really exist, why haven't they shown?
Perhaps it's their will
To protect us still
From a place in the stars that they call home

SCHOOL BULLY

Bruce is the biggest kid in the schoolyard
His mission's to make everybody's life hard
He knows how to pick 'em
And his favorite victim
Is a small boy named Jimmy he calls a retard

Now Jimmy's not stupid or anything like that
But he's thin as a rail, not one ounce of fat
For Bruce he's ideal
'Cause Jimmy won't squeal
Kids in Chicago know what happens to rats

Recess became the most dreadful of times
Jimmy just praying for the next bell to chime
No fun to be found
On the school playground
While Bruce is busy committing his crimes

For so long he's been taking a daily beating
Finally, he talks to his dad while they're eating
His father's aware
But has taken care
To wait for his son to seek out a meeting

Next day he's at school and it's time for recess
He knows what awaits him but Dad put it best
Step up to the plate
Or suffer your fate
Nobody but you puts that heart in your chest

Bruce seeks him out and he's quickly found
Not hiding this time, he is standing his ground
Reaches deep in his guts
Kicks Bruce square in the nuts
Then shatters a knee with a loud cracking sound

So much for the bully who runs home in shame
Though it took quite a while as he's mostly lame
As he tells his tale
The truth becomes pale
In his side you'd think little Jimmy's to blame

Bruce's Dad smacks the sad look from his face
Said how he'd been acting was a family disgrace
He got what was comin'
And not to come runnin'
To him 'cause some kid put him back in his place

This story is true but it's way out of date
If it happened today Jimmy never would skate
Bruce's rights violation
Calls for incarceration
But this all occurred in nineteen fifty-eight

Now Bruce is a senator who's under investigation
For leaking state secrets to an unfriendly nation
And Jimmy's his suit
Now ain't that a hoot
Defending the thug who caused such trepidation

SENIORS

Time passes by and soon age claims us all
There will be changes that we can't forestall
Things worked before
That don't anymore
Muscles and joints, even short-term recall

Eyesight is fading, can't drive to the store
Climbing the stairs has become quite the chore
A back with lumbago
Make such a trip pay so
We keep Ibuprofen in most every drawer

Senior discounts when the early bird sings
The sigh of relief a bowel movement brings
Pepto Bismal
The handicapped stall
These are a few of our favorite things

Empty nest syndrome has become quite a trial
Is keeping this big house really worthwhile?
The children are grown
With kids of their own
No time for us in their hectic lifestyle

Maybe we'll sell and move out to Tucson
Buy our dream house where it's nice and warm
The kids never call
So they've no right to bawl
When they don't inherit 'cause all of it's gone

SHADOW PEOPLE

The Shadow People are a myth, they say
But I believe they exist today
It will unfold
But not as told
No, this will be in a different way

It's said that you may think you've caught
A glimpse of one but when you've sought
To find it out
There's little doubt
What you found wasn't what you thought

I say they're with us day and night
Although a shadow requires the light
But no, not these
They move with ease
Throughout the world just out of sight

The Shadow People are thoughts, you see
The darkest ones from you and me
Although in mind
They often find
Their way to cause catastrophe

In all our wars we've had the means
To halt the march of the death machines
And though we could
We never would
For they were lurking behind the scenes

So if you wonder why some men do
The evil that we bear witness to
Remember well
The tale I tell
Of the Shadow People that live in you

SILVER BALLS

In the Beginning

A million years ago a meteor landed
Leaving its precious cargo stranded
Scattered all around
On the jungle ground
To remain in place as gravity demanded

They began to accumulate the local stone
Around themselves and so they had grown
At different rates
Due solely to fate
As some locations were more or less prone

Spherical shapes grew for thousands of years
When primitive man discovered them here
His artistic cuts
Left long swirling ruts
On every surface his drawings appeared

The Wake-Up Call

East-West tensions are rising ever higher
It seems like war is their only desire
If tempers should flare
Would enemies dare
To blow up this world in a nuclear fire?

The radio telescope in Arecibo
A bowl in the earth of Puerto Rico
Received a new burst
Although not its first
This one had something unexpected in tow

Its frequency was in the expected range
But the subharmonics were very strange
A modulation
Of short duration
Now there's something to study for a change

Could this be a sign of some intelligence?
Given the patterns it surely made sense
They tried to locate
Its source, but too late
The burst quickly ended with indifference

The Awakening

A crowd has gathered in the museum hall
To learn of the legend that fascinates all
The decorated spheres
Found only right here
In Costa Rica lie those mysterious balls

As the tour guide is talking an old lady cries,
"It's getting so hot; I have sweat in my eyes!"
The ball on display
Is no longer grey
But glowing dull red with its temperature rise

Suddenly it cools 'til it's covered in frost
Causing large chunks of its shell to be lost
Now it's vibrating
Thus eliminating
All remaining rock which is finally tossed

What's left is a tiny silver ball on the floor
Three or four inches across and no more
Unknown to those there
It happened everywhere
Three hundred balls lay on jungle and shore

Now the Instructions

Back at Arecibo there's another fast burst
This one is slightly different from the first
Harmonics still there
Unwilling to share
Their secrets before the signal dispersed

Again, it ends quickly, disguising its source
Software will analyze the pattern, of course
But to no avail
They're on a cold trail
The scientists are left to feel the remorse

And Into Action

Back in Costa Rica the balls start to move
Their silver shells now a rainbow of hues
They rise from the ground
Still shining and round
As they go ever higher, they start to diffuse

Now they look just like soap bubble clouds
The show is enjoyed by the museum crowd
Without further delay
Each goes its own way
People watch in awe as long as allowed

Now out of sight each one takes its place
Strategically located in outer space
They circle the globe
Like so many space probes
Connected in a network like a carapace

The War is Foiled

The Eastern bloc countries will not agree
To setting political prisoners free
Dictators taunting
Missiles are launching
Despite the urgent United Nations plea

Soon warheads are flying in both directions
But now unable to make course corrections
They rise much too high
Detonate in the sky
And then disappear from radar detection

GPS satellites are rendered ineffective
How could they all have become defective?
Who's tipping the scale?
When guidance systems fail
Weapons no longer reach their objectives

Without their weapons dictators always fall
It's happening in countries large and small
Uprisings full-blown
Despots overthrown
Governments begin to heed peoples' calls

Message to the People

Once again Arecibo has detected a burst
Scientists hoping that this one's not cursed
Arriving bestowed
With unbreakable code
Just like the second one and like the first

But this time the cipher is easy to break
All are surprised by how little it takes
The sender has asked
That this be broadcast
To the people of Earth for everyone's sake:

We are The Guardians. The shield we have placed around your world will prevent your venture into the stars before you are ready. Until then, it will deny your use of what you call atomic weapons. We are watching.

The Renaissance

It would take a long time to settle the scores
War has a way of leaving festering sores
But they can be healed
And peacemaking appealed
So the people of the Earth took on the chore

The world embarked on a new Golden Age
Treaties were signed so no wars were waged
Weapons dismantled
Disagreements handled
Humans were finally turning the page

New discoveries made in treating disease
Clean energy strides and planting of trees
Reduced carbon emissions
No more nuclear fission
Fusion reactors generate power for free

For a hundred years we have been at peace
Perhaps now our space ships will be released
A launch is attempted
Will it be preempted?
A trip to the moon accomplished in a breeze

The Final Message

Arecibo has long been decommissioned
But telescopes everywhere always listen
At last it is heard
And it's only four words
The Guardians' message is no admonition

WE WISH YOU PEACE

SILVERBACK

The ancient one sits in the shade of a tree
Protected from the sun by a dense canopy
As the little one's tease
He accepts it with ease
In the fierce midday heat no exertion for he

He's father to many but mate to just one
She watches the children engaging in fun
Protective is she
As a mother must be
Patient as well since she's no longer young

The jungle provides everything they require
For anything more, they don't feel a desire
Bed down in a tree
The fruit is all free
If danger approaches there's a simian choir

Gorillas know nothing of human affairs
Here in the jungle that's always been theirs
But man is not known
To leave things alone
Sooner or later, he intrudes everywhere

A chatter arises and the birds all take flight
A human is here but he's still out of sight
Caught unaware
They just sit and stare
As the man with the rifle walks into the light

The silverback faces his unwelcome guest
He roars his outrage and beats on his chest
A shot rings out loud
And the once brave and proud
The ruler of the jungle finds eternal rest

The female is longing to comfort her mate
But instinct warns she'd just share his fate
The youngsters in hiding
Have done her deciding
Better to go now, she knows how to wait

Back at the camp they have laid out a feast
Set for the hunter who conquered the beast
Sodden with ale
He tells them the tale
Embellishing freely to say the very least

Mother and children must work to survive
The odds of success are about one in five
'Cause history shows
How this always goes
But it's not over yet, she's a plan to contrive

She steals into camp in the dead of the night
It's quiet and dark and they've not left a light
Her work is soon done
And when comes the sun
The female's revenge is a most bloody sight

SITTING BULL

In the 1800's the white man came
Upon their land he staked his claim
But these Dakotas
Had been Lakota's
Since a time no one alive could name

No chief was he this holy man
But spiritual leader of his clan
Snow or drought
They sought him out
Whenever trials beset their land

A totem 'round his neck he wore
That no evil spirit could ignore
It let him see
What was to be
And many soldiers is what he saw

As settlers came so armies too
Cabins rose where maize once grew
Pushed away
Not place to stay
Tepees made of skin too few

The time had come at last to fight
And Little Big Horn was the site
Here Custer found
On bloodied ground
They could face his army's might

Alas for long it was not to be
Their prized home lost eventually
Driven forth
Up to the North
But there remain? Oh no, not he

Some time he spent with Buffalo Bill
But soon enough he'd had his fill
With hands in air
Returned to where
The remnants of his tribe lived still

The troopers knew of his rebel past
And new uprisings were forecast
They shot him dead
In chest and head
And so ended Sitting Bull at last

SOUL TRAIN

Tommy Lee Pruitt was a Southern man
Cared for his family by working the land
When the cloud of war
Fell upon his door
It demanded that every man take a stand

A South Carolina lad was Tommy Lee
So he signed up with the Confederacy
With rifle and ball
Tommy stood tall
A man has to fight if he means to be free

It was Pittsburgh Landing in Tennessee
Where Tommy first engaged the enemy
Although not the worst
It was one of the first
The Battle of Shiloh it would come to be

Smoke filled the sky as the battle ensued
The enemies struggled in a bloody feud
Confederate sons
Fell to Union guns
Bluecoats as well saw the bodies accrue

Tommy is groggy, slow to come around
He remembers falling on the battleground
Though he feels no pain
His shirt is blood-stained
And the stump of a leg is securely bound

As Tommy looks around he tries in vain
To see where he is but his eyes must strain
Sunlight filters through
And obscures the view
But Tommy suspects that he's on a train

The rocking motion as it rides the track
Soothes his body when he leans back
He's sure it's a train
But then again
Where is that sound of the clickety-clack?

The fog lifts a bit, now Tommy can see
There are others in the car sitting silently
All soldiers are they
Both bluecoat and grey
And every one wounded to some degree

He sees the scars of the battle they fought
"Why aren't they dead?", he sadly thought
Their wounds are extreme
Yet somehow, they seem
At peace while riding this iron juggernaut

His vision is playing strange tricks on him
The light in the car is bright and then dim
With each flash of light
He loses his sight
When it's regained what he sees is grim

There are fewer soldiers now than before
Tommy looks around but he sees no door
Where are they going?
Then a flash of knowing
I'm on the last ride for casualties of war

This train doesn't have any destination
It will never stop at some railway station
It's the train of souls
That forever rolls
Transporting passengers to their salvation

One after another the soldiers depart
'Til there's no one but Tommy left in the car
Then the flash of light
And Tommy's upright
No longer wounded and stronger of heart

He's standing in a field of newly sown corn
This is his farm and the place he was born
It's nearing sunset
And he has no regrets
Looking over the things he defended in war

His good wife is standing by the cabin door
He imagines the children playing on the floor
Now he sees they're OK
He'll be on his way
Another bright flash and Tommy's no more

TAM BIET, VIETNAM

Now fifty years gone yet I never have told
Of a time I recall that turned young men old
Some now choose to hide
Their feelings inside
The years might erase the memories they hold

But time's not the healer it's cracked up to be
For once you have seen you can never unsee
Those things that survive
Like bees in a hive
Buzz around in the brain in a bid to be free

Compound surrounded by sandbags and wire
Sentries afforded a clear field of fire
But sappers delight
In entering at night
The smallest of holes is all they require

They say that I'm "in the rear with the gear"
Sounds hollow to me with Charlie so near
It's easy to see
The DMZ
So from where I am standing it seems insincere

We always had access to alcohol
Generously consumed by most if not all
It's best to be numb
The night's yet to come
Rockets and mortars are guaranteed to fall

When they fly in we are driven like sheep
Into the bunkers in an effort to keep
Alive 'til we hear
Them sound the all clear
Little hope left there will be any sleep

Eighteen years old and far from his home
Only her letters help him feel less alone
But the girl left behind
Changes her mind
So he swallows his rifle to make her atone

A hard charging captain is driving his men
If they're to survive he must harden them
But one of his crew
Answers, "No, thank you!"
With a fragmentation grenade in his tent

No such thing as a secure piece of ground
Win it then lose it and around and around
'Til they finally decide
To just let it slide
Blood washes away as the rain pours down

tam biet means goodbye in Vietnamese
When I first left there I said it with ease
But not true, it seams
I go back there in dreams
So all I can hope for is, "*tam biet, please!*"

THE ANGRY GHOST

Around the world local customs are varied
Of how and when their loved ones are buried
For some several days
Or perhaps right away
But for most it has to be more or less hurried

On one small island dead are not left in state
But buried that day as their custom dictates
Left in shallow graves
So they can be saved
And safely recovered before the festival date

It's believed their loved ones will favor them
And bless the ground while they lie therein
Next year when they sow
The taro will grow
Large and starchy with sweet leaves and skin

They reserve the last three days of each year
To celebrate the ancestors whom they hold dear
Their island is small
And they need it all
So the use of a funeral pyre is most austere

Men's lives are short but ghosts live forever
They remain unaffected by war or weather
But their shallow graves
Make them so depraved
They hassle the living just for pure pleasure

Until they're celebrated at the end of the year
Fishing nets are cut and cattle dung smeared
On dugout canoes
With leaves of bamboo
And falling coconuts lead to ghostly cheers

There's one in the tribe who everyone knows
Will not be so playful when he finally goes
Palu hates everyone
And so people shun
But members of the tribe must be disposed

The day finally comes when Palu is dead
Throughout the tribe not a single tear is shed
But what evil tricks
Might Palu inflict?
Fear of his revenge fills the village with dread

A tribe meeting is held to discuss what to do
This island was never a good place for Palu
There's a rocky atoll
Where old Palu's soul
Should leave us alone until we burn him too

So his body is floated out into the bay
And covered with rocks until comes the day
When festival's held
Then we'll be compelled
To bring him back home, it's always our way

Life went back to normal or so it seemed
But Palu's ghost had concocted a scheme
Fishermen return
With looks of concern
The nets come up empty, a sight never seen

The taro are beginning to rot in the ground
Blame for these troubles can only be found
In the ghost of Palu
And he's left a clue
The whole village watches as his hut burns down

This can't go on because the people will die
So Palu is returned and given a place to lie
A fine bamboo bower
Covered in flowers
Is placed by his grave to please Palu's eye

Soon things improve although slowly at first
All are not sure that they've seen the worst
But nets fill again
And taro regain
Sweet leaves and roots in a welcome rebirth

When festival comes there's a beautiful pyre
The dead are placed on it for all to admire
Palu is praised
As the fire is raised
Hope is rekindled as the flames rise higher

THE BOXER

I am a fighter, that's all I can do
Once a contender between me and you
The licensing board
Says I can't box no more
They won't say why so I don't got a clue

I once almost won the middleweight crown
'Cuz I kept knocking the other guy down
But he wouldn't stay
And all I can say's
When I woke up I was flat on the ground

Doc says I fight now and I will be dead
Got a big tuna inside o' my head
Nasty old thing
Came from the ring
Eyesight is fuzzy and hands feel like lead

I live at the gym and got a small room
Empty spit buckets and push a big broom
Ain't got no wife
So this is my life
Sweaty ol' towels and jock strap perfume

But fightin's my game and I can't let it be
There's only one way for me to be free
I'll sneak out at dark
Go down to da park
And let some street fighter end it for me

THE BROKEN SPOKE

The Broken Spoke is my favorite bar
Close to home so I don't need a car
As honky-tonks go
It's only so-so
Then I'm a guy who drinks from a jar

With the wobbly stools it's easy to fall
The closer it gets to time for last call
They ain't got no band
But a drunk fiddlin' man
Plays when he's had enough alcohol

I've seen a few folks cryin' in their beer
Over some lost love who's no longer here
Dumped and now lonely
For that one and only
But all of that booze does little to cheer

Waylon came here to recall an old love
Reminiscin' heals wounds, well, sort of
What are the perks
When nothin' else works
What's one to do when push comes to shove?

Now I don't judge but it still makes me think
Some just don't care how far down they sink
I've heard Waylon's song
So I might be wrong
But my only reason for coming here's to drink

THE DANVERS PARTY

This story is fictional although historically accurate insofar as the trials and hardships faced by those settlers who ventured West along the Oregon Trail go. The Danvers were typical of the brave souls who gambled on a chance for a new life and fresh opportunities. Also accurate is the fact that a Presbyterian missionary named Elijah Wood did, in fact, make the journey to the Oregon Territory and return to lead a second expedition in the following year, albeit not this particular one.

The story begins in Tennessee some time in 1842. The Danvers, like many other tenant farmers, grow more and more frustrated with the landlords and their lots in life.

East Tennessee farmland was owned by a few
The families who worked it unfortunately knew
Though they worked the land
It would be the rich man
Who'd reap the benefit of the crops they grew

On one of these farms lived the Danvers family
John was the father and a strong man was he
He had two young boys
A daughter who's a joy
And he loved his wife Melinda unconditionally

Will was 13 and worked with Dad in the fields
Melissa, 11, helped Mom with the meals
Jimmy, just 9
Was only assigned
To feed Molly the dog and grind the cornmeal

All that they owned were their sleeping beds
Two horses and a wagon with a cover shed
Table and some chairs
Candlesticks a pair
Dishes, cutlery and Mom's sewing threads

Melinda would teach the kids by candlelight
When all of the chores were done every night
Their letters were taught
Though no books were bought
A dirt floor and stick that mom used to write

One day as a neighbor was talking to John
He spoke of a Western migration that's on
A man can lay claim
To land he can tame
And bequeath to his heirs after he's gone

He speaks to Melinda at the end of the day
Afraid his enthusiasm might lead him astray
"I'm asking of you,
too good to be true?"
His down-to-earth wife will have the last say

Melinda has heard the same talk hereabout
Women she knows express serious doubts
That land is too wild
No place for a child
To be sure going West is a dangerous route

But she must consider the way they live now
A brighter tomorrow this life won't allow
No future for the kids
But to do as they're bid
Destined to always pull another man's plow

Melinda thought silently how this could play
She knew very soon she must have her say
Should our heads stay level
Or dance with the devil?
She spoke to her husband the following day

"Our children are bright and do lessons well.
What they might become no one can foretell.
But here on this land
they must work for the man.
All their descendants will be under his spell."

"If you believe our destiny lies in the West
we all will go with you and do our very best
to tame that wild land
with our roughened hands
and hope that our sacrifice is ultimately blest."

John has learned that others are preparing
To make the journey no matter how daring
They too have been slaves
And it's freedom they crave
Landlords are greedy and just plain uncaring

Last year a group of settlers drove out West
One of their number returned and expressed
A willingness to guide
Across the Great Divide
Any hardy souls who would take on the quest

We must cross the Rockies before it snows
Elijah Wood will be our guide and he knows
It's his experience
That will be our defense
So he's the trail boss and what he says goes

The day has come and the wagon is packed
The horses may tire so some will walk in back
Little Jimmy and Will
Are up for the thrill
Molly is with them, her tongue hanging slack

The wagons all gather just outside of town
Throwin' up dust 'til it turns the sky brown
They're off with a fury
For Elm Grove, Missouri
Jumping off point for that promised ground

None of these farmers have ever been away
From the work they do for more than a day
At first relocation
Felt like a vacation
But all had to walk at least part of the way

Soon the long days began to take their toll
Children tire easily and must be consoled
But so many miles
Are needed meanwhile
Each may soon fade but wagons had to roll

The Danvers pushed on by helping one another
Will has grown into his role as big brother
Missy's feeling down
And Jimmy wears a frown
All feel the stress but find comfort in Mother

For the journey planned this is the safest part
They're in settled territory right from the start
If any can't last
He must find out fast
The trip requires stamina but also takes heart

The trail boss says get to know your neighbors
Sooner or later, everyone will need a favor
Loan a cup of cornmeal
Fix a broken wagon wheel
Pitch in as midwife when a mother's in labor

As the sun is setting the wagons are circled
As a means of defense this is now universal
There's little danger now
But they must know how
It will soon be required and so the rehearsal

Campfires are lit and the meals are prepared
Friendships are made and stories compared
They post guards each night
Around the campsite
Again, this is practice and no man is spared

Then a few weeks later their first destination
Elm Grove, Missouri offers some relaxation
But only for a day
Then back on their way
To reach the Rockies before snow formation

And now the most difficult journey begins
Fraught with danger from beginning to end
The long road ahead
Is riddled with dread
The Kansas Territory is treacherous and vast

Water will be the most difficult thing to find
Elijah Wood the trail boss comes to remind
"Be careful and ration
but do show compassion.
Your cattle and oxen come second in line."

They set out to find the dream they all share
After many days the drudgery starts to wear
The scene never changes
Hot temper exchanges
Are taking a toll on the travelers' welfare

But Elijah has news that brings on a smile
They're in Nebraska not a hundred miles
From Fort Laramie
Four days, maybe three
To water the animals and rest for a while

After two days of rest and wagon repairs
They set out again in the hot summer air
Still heading North and West
As Elijah knows is best
Water barrels filled with Platte River fare

Suddenly Elijah calls a halt to the train
There are buffalo grazing out on the plain
The best hunters ride
At Elijah's side
The meat and the hides will help to sustain

Many are killed and as the wagons close in
Elijah has taught them to butcher and skin
The bounty is shared
And supper prepared
Most never ate buffalo but will do so again

With their bellies full they continue the trek
Though some of the wagons are rolling wrecks
There's no time to pause
They'll go on because
Snow in the Rockies will show no respect

They're in Sioux country and Elijah knows
How silent they are as they stalk buffalo
And now he has sensed
Their stealthy presence
They can track us unseen wherever we go

They haven't attacked so that's a good sign
With white men here they're not always kind
The soldiers are near
For now, that strikes fear
But they could quite easily change their minds

Scouts are killing many buffalo to support
Soldiers and their families at Western forts
Herds are being thinned
For meat and for skins
Some are even killing them just for the sport

Elijah knows the Sioux depend on the herds
Wiping them out means violence conferred
The Sioux would attack
To drive us all back
It's best to leave some boiling pots unstirred

Many days later they have reached Fort Hall
Missy's been sick although brave thru it all
But she's getting worse
Despite Mother nurse
They hope there's a doctor on whom they can call

It's cholera she has and the outlook is bleak
They try mightily but she grows ever weak
The end's no surprise
In two days, she dies
There isn't any solace the Danvers can seek

This journey has not been safe in the least
Their practice has been if one is deceased
Burial on the plain
Run over by the train
To hide their scent from scavenging beasts

Elijah is sorry but we must be on our way
We just can't afford to remain another day
Melinda can't go on
Now that Missy's gone
But what would they do if they were to stay?

It turns out Fort Hall has a proper graveyard
It's better than the trail but it still will be hard
We could visit her here
She'd always be near
And we swore our family would not be apart

Soldiers have reported there's good farmland
Along the Snake River, as yet it's unmanned
Drive in some stakes
That's all it takes
Work your own farm as you've always planned

So Missy's interred in the graveyard nearby
John surveys a parcel that caught his eye
A hundred-acre plot
Is marked on the spot
And at Fort Hall the claim is legally applied

The wagon will be their home for a while
So near the Snake River the land is fertile
They've brought their own seed
To provide for their needs
Out here they must each become versatile

The horses are rested and it's time to plow
For a harvest this year they must begin now
It takes many days
To plow and plant maize
They'll start a sod house when time will allow

Winter is near but the house is not done
The corn shines yellow in the Autumn sun
The stalks will provide
When laid out and dried
Sheaves for the roof as proper insulation

As the harvest begins a small party of Sioux
With no warning at all comes riding into view
The Danvers have known
They were never alone
And now this group shows up out of the blue

One who must be the leader rides up close
Waves his arm around then looks at his host
A young brave jumps down
Lays a blanket on the ground
Hands skins to John and returns to his post

Without a word spoken the deal is made
Blankets and skins for John's corn in trade
The leader makes a fist
And holds it to his chest
As John imitates him the group rides away

Next day a Sioux woman arrives at the door
She signals Melinda and they sit on the floor
His wife bids him go
There's much work and so
John and Will depart to resume their chores

The Sioux woman teaches Melinda to tan
Their buffalo skins and on the other hand
Melinda can treat
The fat from the meat
To fashion candles which are in high demand

The sod house is completed soon thereafter
Sheaves of corn stalks are tied to the rafters
And now on most nights
By soft candlelight
At long last erupts the sounds of laughter

Missy's long gone and they miss her still
But their lives must go on and so they will
The Winter is brutal
But complaining futile
They'll survive though the journey travels uphill

As time went by the friendship grew strong
Sioux and settlers actually getting along
The Sioux tongue was learned
And thus in return
English found its way into the Sioux throng

John and Melinda would eventually die
A new house was built, the sod house beside
A suitable place
A family to raise
Will took a Sioux maiden as his new bride

Soon there were children running around
Jimmy and Will grew used to the sound
Of laughter and crying
Found it gratifying
Their house turned into a child's playground

Will needed bullets and the Fort needed corn
So an uneasy trade agreement was born
But to wed a redskin
They thought was a sin
When he arrived he was held up to scorn

Jimmy turned into a smart farming man
Greatly increasing the size of their land
By staking new claims
Made the Danvers name
Known far and wide as a respected brand

In eighteen sixty-eight a treaty was signed
Requiring the Sioux to leave their land behind
A mass migration
Onto reservations
Ethnic cleansing of the white man's design

The soldiers arrive to take their family away
Many are the same ones they see every day
But Jimmy and Will
Refuse to stand still
And fall to the onslaught the very same day

Their land is now forfeit and open to claim
Some other settler can now make his name
Standing on the graves
Of those who would brave
To defy a government devoid of all shame

THE GUARDIAN

A world that orbits a bright yellow star
Is light years away so it's much too far
Although we can't go
You might like to know
That life on this planet is truly bizarre

Its only season is temperate and mild
A near circular orbit is the reason why
Rains on occasion
Balance the equation
And never throw the ecosystem awry

It has rivers and lakes all over the place
A large ocean covers a third of its face
But all the flat land
Is made up of strands
Woven together in a pattern, like lace

Forming a huge mat many meters deep
An organic lifeform with secrets to keep
The planet's backbone
And Guardian of the Krone
To the casual eye it looks to be asleep

Many small creatures inhabit this mat
It nourishes them but there is tit-for-tat
When the creatures' lives end
They're absorbed by the strands
The symbiotic cycle is as simple as that

Yet another creature inhabits this place
Its name was given it by a predator race
They call them the Krone
And invade their home
When they are able to traverse the space

Imagine a tree stump about four feet tall
It has two long arms but no hands at all
No ears, eyes or nose
At least none that shows
Like a snail it uses its one foot to crawl

When one is chosen to bear an offspring
Strands rise up around it and gently cling
Guardian makes the choice
Krones haven't a voice
A seed is planted and a new life it brings

After a short gestation a single egg is laid
It's covered with strands in several braids
Strand binds to strand
As Guardian commands
A type of maternal connection is made

Guardian will feed and protect the Krone
Until such time as it becomes full grown
Then the strands relax
In the final act
Freeing the Krone to go off on its own

The predators have come for many years
But they're mostly not able to travel here
The distance too great
And so they must wait
'Til the planets' two orbits bring them near

Guardian knows of the killing of the Krone
Their bodies are used as food back home
Population control
Is Guardian's role
But it can't keep up now, not on its own

What has happened to cause the change?
They're staying longer and that is strange
Never mind the facts
The Guardian must act
To bring the population back into range

We on the outside can make calculations
To figure the planets' proximity variations
If the time they are near
Increases every year
It would explain the rise in Krone predation

Guardian begins by pulling invaders down
Into its labyrinth of strands underground
It's held firmly therein
While small creatures begin
Devouring the invader from outside and in

The predators can see they stand no chance
Having been trapped in this deadly dance
Ships are readied to leave
When escape is achieved
They race for home with no second glance

It'll take many years to replenish the Krone
Guardian works hard creating new clones
The predator disaster
Makes it work faster
Until enough seeds have finally been sown

When its work is completed, it will hibernate
Though not fully asleep as it must incubate
The eggs that were laid
Across all its braids
Until they are grown The Guardian will wait

THE GUNFIGHTER

He walks away from the man he's just killed
Slow on the draw but drunk and strong-willed
A scourge on the town
Now lying face down
In the dirt and his blood just recently spilled

This town's just another like all of the rest
Its people are trying to tame the Wild West
Good people they are
But to carry a star
Storekeepers and farriers can't pass the test

So most have no sheriff to manage the peace
Lawlessness then creates a sense of unease
In such an event
The word must be sent
For one who can rid the town of disease

The gunfighter knows he must travel alone
Forsaking all those whom he ever has known
If any distraction
Slows his reaction
That puddle of blood could well be his own

Everything he owns is carried on his horse
Saddle and blanket and his guns, of course
He has just one aim
One day to lay claim
To a spread of his own up in the far North

Cold weather suits him, then there's his name
Mostly unknown there is his gunslinging fame
No more gun battles
Just a few cattle
And a wild horse or two he can quietly tame

He's always collected his bounties in gold
Carried in his saddlebags it's never been sold
Good in any exchange
Even out on the range
He'll use it to purchase his longed-for freehold

One day he knows he's lost that keen edge
Now he must do what he long ago pledged
He saddles his horse
And turns to the North
Hoping to leave behind memories of the dead

Montana Territory is where he settles down
Bought a few acres of good grazing ground
He's hung up his guns
And the fencing is done
For a string of wild ponies, he recently found

Early in the morning he crawls out of his bed
Hoping to bring the horses back to his spread
But he's met at the door
With a deafening roar
As a hail of bullets tears his body to shreds

The posse had followed his trail many months
Lost it and picked it up again more than once
He killed the wrong man
A cattle ranch hand
Shot thru the window of Castner's storefront

Although a gunfighter might live to grow old
Escaping his past takes a lot more than gold
The deeds he has done
In a life ruled by guns
Will one way or other at last take their toll

THE HOLIDAYS

Thanksgiving came with food everywhere
Being told to moderate is blatantly unfair
The doctor knows best
But you know the rest
I ate so much I required a wheelchair

The gift list for Christmas was way too long
Expensive tech toys and fighting the throng
When Black Friday came
It was more of the same
I thought I'd go early but man was I wrong!

Next my wife wanted a huge Christmas tree
Went out to the woods, just my axe and me
After two hours of chopping
I gave up and went shopping
Three hundred dollars excluding delivery

So now we've got needles all over the floor
Then I tried putting a wreath on the door
When hammer hit thumb
My whole arm went numb
We're not displaying that thing anymore

The time came for me to shovel the snow
Off of the driveway while it's twenty below
Brushed off the advice
To watch out for ice
I slipped on the stuff and broke my big toe

Slid down the drive slamming into a truck
Broke my left leg and just for good luck
Momentum on my side
Continued the slide
Under the truck while forgetting to duck

The driver looked at me and asked if I'd sign
For the load he brought 'cuz it was all mine
But my right arm was stuck
Still under his truck
Asked my wife to do it if she wouldn't mind

As I'm lying in bed with my leg up in wires
My wife rushes in, happy tears in her eyes
"My family is here!"
Am I supposed to cheer?
I can't think of a more unwanted surprise

Finally, it's over and we take down the tree
At least I know the city will haul it for me
But no, that's not true
Disposal's up to you
So I got a ticket for leaving it by the street

I'm giving up holidays for the rest of my life
No more turkeys, retired my carving knife
Next time it's cold here
We're gonna disappear
It's holidays in Hawaii for me and my wife

THE MEDICINE CHEST

An old man lay dying his son sits beside
The one living heir of the MacIver pride
A strapping young man
He's the last of his clan
The future of the name is his to provide

Father has left him a small wooden chest
Ornately adorned with the MacIver crest
Strange it's not locked
But on top of the box
A message is written in Old English text:

A tea for thy heart and one for thy brain
Another one comforts thy stomach pain
A MacIver may use
The tea once so choose
Then never may ye open this chest again

"Heed the warning!", his father implores
Then silently leaves him to utter no more
The small chest in hand
Ian buries the man
Who left him so little yet whom he adored

Our Ian, it seems, was a fan of the brew
Never just one, always more than a few
Night after night
In the pub 'til first light
To work after sleep, just an hour or two

One morning he suffers a major migraine
It's the alcohol's doing, indescribable pain
He remembers the box
Without any locks
A tea for thy heart and one for thy brain

He looks 'round his flat 'til he finally finds
The warning on top is still there to remind
Brews the tea for the head
Goes straight off to bed
Arises with a whole new presence of mind

Cured of the pain he resumes his lifestyle
Back in the pub after just a short while
Drinking and smoking
Laughing and joking
Courting disaster with an idiotic smile

Ian doubles over in total surprise
The pain in his chest is increasing in size
He grabs the box but
It's now tightly shut
And it will not open no matter he tries

Found with the little box still in his clutch
It easily opens with just a light touch
No markings on the chest
So they just had to guess
Why did an old box of tea mean so much?

THE OLD OAK TREE

It was already old when the settlers arrived
Fair weather and foul the oak tree survived
Bending with the wind
Come Winter it thinned
Adaptation the key that allowed it to thrive

The old tree saw a nation erupt in civil war
Asking itself, "What are they fighting for?"
One keeps his slaves
The other one braves
To challenge the practice that he so abhors

Once it was known as The Hangin' Tree
A dark time in history most folks can agree
But all things must pass
Thought some not so fast
That memory still lingers for all of us to see

It wore yellow ribbons thru both world wars
Waiting for countries to settle their scores
But nothing was learned
By nations that burned
Aggression continued for many years more

Sons who once played in its protective shade
Sent off to fight when a new war was made
Vietnam and Korea
"Wouldn't wanna be ya!"
Draft dodgers yelled as sad mothers prayed

Then we had Iraq and Afghanistan
The tree dons the yellow ribbons once again
More blood was spilled
Sons and daughters killed
And we're left to wonder if it will ever end

That old tree remembers my family and me
We lived in a house on the same property
Shaded barbecues
An afternoon snooze
Beneath the protection of it vast canopy

An old, worn-out tire someone threw away
And a long piece of rope only slightly frayed
Made a swing in the tree
For my brother and me
Which afforded us so many hours of play

We wanted a treehouse but Mom was afraid
We'd both break our necks and so she forbade
Dad would have built it
But after Mom killed it
No mention of that was thereafter made

We called in a company to trim the old tree
It was hanging over another one's property
They never complained
But as Mom explained
Good neighbors have a certain responsibility

I drive by and see that the old house is gone
The tree is surrounded by a manicured lawn
A little girl swings
In that old rubber ring
That after all of these years is still hanging on

One day the leaders of the nations will see
Only through peace can all people be free
I won't be around
Layin' long in the ground
But I hope that old tree lives to see it for me

THE PLANO POSSE

Larry and Jimmy and Corky and Dwight
And Toad so named for a large overbite
Idolize the Lone Ranger
Who rides into danger
On TV channel 4 every Saturday night

Best friends at 11 they love to ride down
To the old train graveyard outside of town
They don't have to share
As nobody goes there
Just an old hobo who's always around

His wizened face is bearded and scarred
Suggesting a life of times lean and hard
He gets by on his own
So they leave him alone
Racing their bikes around the trainyard

At dusk they patrol the ol' neighborhood
Like the Lone Ranger they aim to do good
But keeping the peace
Is a job for police
So leave it to them as they know they should

They rescued a kitten stuck high in a tree
Took a blind lady shopping at the new A&P
Poor little girl lost
A busy street crossed
Seen safely home by the Plano Posse

BOB BRIGGS

Corky has a dog who had puppies in May
It's been 8 weeks now so what do you say
The Train Man's alone
But a dog of his own
Would give him some company every day

He uttered not a word, just nodded his head
Some things are known, no words being said
A tear in his eye
As they waved him goodbye
His beard now concealing a face turning red

The Posse continued to race at the site
As the puppy grew older it took great delight
In chasing them 'round
The trampled down ground
The old man watching in the fading daylight

The day finally came when the old hobo died
Dog and The Posse all stood there and cried
The police came and found
Near the man on the ground
A torn scrap of paper he'd left by his side:

plez thank thoz
boyz 4 my dog
hez the onle frend
i ever had

THE REFUGEE

Master Sergeant Hyde is a well-seasoned vet
He's on his sixth tour and it's not over yet
His nerves forged in war
But what's it all for?
Asking the question only serves to upset

He walks through the ruins of a Syrian town
Leveled at night when the bombs came down
A house with two walls
Which somehow didn't fall
Gets his attention with a whimpering sound

A scared and trembling little girl was inside
So tired and frightened she no longer cried
Her parents both dead
Laying there head-to-head
On the floor with the little girl sitting beside

He picks her up slowly 'cuz she cannot stay
Her small arms curl around him as if to say
"Please help me big man,
I know that you can."
And he melts like butter on a hot summer day

A wash and a checkup by a doctor who said
"Her health is OK but with both parents' dead,
her future's unsure,
for that I've no cure."
But Hyde has a different idea in his head

He Skypes with his wife every evening at ten
Because so many time zones separate them
But the girl won't let go
Of her savior and so
His wife sees her and so he speaks of it then

For these many years they've longed for a child
But it's tough to manage across all those miles
And now fate has seen
Fit to answer their dream
Refuting that to which they'd been reconciled

They agree over Skype but the path will be long
Both sides of the world must each remain strong
There'll be many delays
But we'll find a way
We know where this lovely orphan child belongs

And so it began from both sides of the sea
The effort to bring the girl home to safety
After months of red tape
They could finally escape
They're met at the airport by the mother-to-be

He's seen her home safely but he cannot stay
His tour won't be over for many more days
A brief respite there
Placing her in Mom's care
Then back to the war and the game he must play

This tour's finally over and still no cease fire
After twenty and some he decides to retire
He sees in hindsight
It was never his fight
So he puts in his papers and leaves the quagmire

He watches his family as they play on the floor
The questions once posed aren't asked anymore
They look up at him
And flash a big grin
At least something good has emerged from the war

THE STARLIGHT

The 50's and 60's were my good old days
We proved rock'n'roll was not just a phase
Wore white tee shirts
And poodle skirts
Sock hops featured the latest dance craze

High school jackets with sports letters sewn
You had to be a jock so I didn't own
Cheerleaders yearned
For those who had earned
Big men on campus was how they were known

TV's had rabbit ears not satellite or cable
Nothing we bought carried warning labels
Car hops on skates
Where we took our dates
And played the juke box from every table

Chopping our cars and combing our hair
With Brylcreem to uphold a swept back flair
A new transistor
For my big sister
Pedal pushers skin-tight to elicit a stare

The drive-in movie's the best memory of all
With a screen that was well over 50 feet tall
Concession stand
A Saturday band
The Starlight was open from Spring until Fall

None of us had any money back then
We'd hide in the trunk and try to sneak in
A stern lesson taught
If you ever got caught
But of course we'd always attempt it again

Weeknights a dollar for the whole family
Brothers and sisters and parents and me
I thought of my friends
But then in the end
A family together was the best place to be

Summers and Winters went on day by day
Then all of a sudden life got in the way
Boys turned to men
That old cycle again
The joy that was youth got lost in the fray

The Starlight is closed now so many years
Bulldozed and leveled so it's now a Sears
But I'll always miss
Where I got my first kiss
The corn dogs, popcorn and Hires root beer

Don't live in the past
But try to recall
Those things that should last
The best times of all

THE TALISMAN

I'm just an old man in a rocking chair
A shawl on my lap against the night air
Outside on the lawn
I'll sit until dawn
Another day passed in a life so unfair

I've outlived my kids and their kids too
How I'm still here is amazing but true
I fought in three wars
Still wonder what for
Lost many friends who didn't pull thru

I grew up next to a gypsy campsite
Played with the kids until the last light
One day they were gone
Time came to move on
Romani unwelcome in city folks' sight

But before they left a friend I adored
Gave me a present, all she could afford
Protection for me
'Til next time she'd see
A small talisman on a tan leather cord

It's not so much that I'm superstitious
But tempting fate is never judicious
And So "What the heck?"
It stayed 'round my neck
Besides it was never anyone's business

First World War II and armed with a gun
I was off to fight against the Rising Sun
We settled the score
On Corregidor
When it was over, I hoped we were done

Next came the Communists itching to fight
One more soldier versus Red Army might
So many were killed
In those Korean hills
Again, I was lucky and came thru it in spite

But men never tire of war, it would seem
And there I was joining another new team
During Vietnam
Many bought the farm
My lucky escapes haunt all of my dreams

I was finally too old to fight anymore
So I retired and set out looking for
The gypsies I knew
Way back in my youth
I hope they can tell me why I survived war

I'm sure they have covered a lot of ground
And they're very good at not being found
But once again luck
Had found me and struck
I stumbled upon them near Puget Sound

My talisman, they said, had cared for me
But it's also a burden that I've yet to see
No matter you try
It won't let you die
But if you bury it deep it will set you free

Out on the horizon a soft pinkish glow
The time is approaching when I will go
"When the sun doth rise
will come your demise"
For the talisman is deep in the earth below

THE TRUCKER'S WIFE

Her husband's a trucker and seldom at home
The kids old enough she can leave them alone
Nights out with the girls
In the honky-tonk world
Longing for the love he has lately not shown

She knows the reputation of highway truck stops
After 10 or 12 hours chewing up the blacktop
A knock on the door
He welcomes the whore
A half hour of pleasure with no need to shop

A dusty ranch hand every Saturday night
Scrapes off the dirt and seeks out the lights
He's made his way here
For a dance and cold beer
Maybe get lucky with some weekend delight

He has little money, just enough for the brew
But even poor ranch hands look for love too
Should he take a chance?
Maybe ask her to dance?
Can she understand what he's going thru?

She's with her friends but looks in his direction
He catches her eye and smiles with affection
His smile is returned
One thing he has learned
Nothing to lose when you're used to rejection

She excuses herself to go powder her nose
A nod as she passes and the cowboy follows
Where the hallway is dim
She whispers to him
How will we do this so nobody knows?

It's Saturday night, all the hands are in town
Back at his bunkhouse there's no one around
They'll each leave alone
Drive away on their own
She'll fake illness, say she wants to lie down

For an hour or so they forget everything else
Making the best of the cards they were dealt
A husband who cheats
The intense desert heat
For days they relive the joy that they felt

The relationship continues in a secrecy shroud
But cheap motels don't make them feel proud
Her friends ask her why
She doesn't come by
Says she's lost interest in the bars and crowds

Each finds pleasure in their one-night stands
But both know a future can never be planned
They'll have to make do
With this life, these two
A widow to the road and a dirt-poor ranch hand

THING

Pinto Flats, Texas is a tired little town
Businesses here have mostly shut down
The new interstate
Determined their fate
Now hardly anyone ever comes around

Traffic control is an amber flashing light
Which signals to no one all day and night
The one open store
Sells gas, little more
The diner serves locals but custom is slight

There once was a Stuckey's on the old highway
A motorist's rest stop back in the day
But now it's all gone
And time marches on
The good old days is now just a cliche'

Too small for a sheriff or any lawman
Still Pinto Flats does the best that it can
They're part of a county
But no Texas mountie
Ever comes around there as a regular plan

Pinto Flats, though, has a criminal history
Its unsolved murders still remain a mystery
Seven victims known
But they're not alone
More are missing but there's no inquiry

Next to Stuckey's was The Thing Museum
Folks would stop and pay money to see 'em
The two-headed snake
And others were fake
But Thing was so real you could almost feel 'im

The creature was short, only four feet tall
Skinny and pink and completely bald
You've heard looks can kill
Well, he filled the bill
His sharp pointed teeth made the skin crawl

Locals used to say that he got out at night
And killed all those people with a single bite
The missing, they said
Were assumed to be dead
Left in the woods at some hidden campsite

A retired Texas Ranger named Samuel Bell
Heard of the killings so he stopped for a spell
The diner's the place
To learn of the case
So he might as well have a nice meal as well

The folks aren't bashful and tell him the tale
A story that's turned quite a few tourists pale
He thinks it's absurd
But something occurred
Murder was committed on a terrible scale

Bell's now determined to seek out the facts
The locals warn him he could be attacked
They all wish him well
And are happy as hell
They know for certain he will never be back

The beast must be fed for the town to survive
So here in the diner the tale's kept alive
The skeptical ones
Provide the most fun
They enter the woods thinking it's all contrived

THIS TOWN

Didn't stop here on purpose, I ran out of gas
I'll sleep in the truck, not the first time or last
My money's gone too
And I ain't got a clue
How to keep running away from my past

I was raised in Kentucky way back in the hills
We kept to ourselves, had no problems until
A government man
Says we don't own our land
We had to move off but we stayed on it still

Next thing you know they attack us with guns
Shot one of 'em dead and my Papa said run
So I jumped in my truck
Ever trustin' to luck
And high-tailed it out, never lookin' back once

Many back roads and small towns on my way
Workin' odd jobs and getting by day to day
I must keep my head low
Wherever I go
For now, I am safe and not government prey

This town that I'm in's a wide spot in the road
Out here in West Texas my journey has slowed
Not much to see here
Cowboys drinkin' Pearl beer
They invite me to join them and lighten my load

I tell them about getting kicked off our land
Except for the part where I shot that G-man
In these parts, they say
You don't take land away
From a man just doin' the best that he can

I ask if there's work I can do for my feed
If I can wash dishes the diner has a need
I scrub the pots clean
'Til they sparkle and gleam
There's a permanent job if I am agreed

This town is remote and friendly, I've found
Maybe it's time that I finally settled down
They're still lookin' for me
But these folks let me be
I've made up my mind to remain in this town

Sold my old truck to buy a small piece of land
I've got no machines so must work it by hand
It doesn't yield much
Peppers, okra and such
And my job at the diner helps me stick to plan

I learned that my family would hold out until
The Feds decided to move in for the kill
There was no happy ending
They all died defending
The life they had built in the Kentucky hills

TIME TO DIE

Most of us try to do the best we can
Paulie O'Connor was that kind of man
He worked every day
And brought home his pay
Caring for his family was his only plan

He had a job but you know how it goes
Car has bald tires, kids need new clothes
Summer vacation
Mortgage inflation
It's a hectic life but it's what they chose

In spite of all this they saved a wee bit
They knew rainy days were liable to hit
What they put away
Wouldn't help a tough day
Enough for a drizzle and that's about it

Maggie had a part time job at Wal*Mart
Collecting and returning shopping carts
The kids were in class
And the time went fast
It made her feel she was doing her part

Paulie was never the type to complain
But lately he was having stomach pains
He'd been eating less
Energy depressed
A bit of weight loss he couldn't explain

But he put off the doctor due to the bills
Said he was fine and relied on pain pills
But soon it took more
Two, three and then four
Until Maggie caught him getting refills

He finally agreed to get it checked out
The battery of tests soon left little doubt
Not a good answer
Paulie had cancer
News the family could have done without

When he is told what the treatment entails
Paulie and Maggie turn six shades of pale
The chemo ain't free
And no guarantee
Paulie was thinking to balance the scale

What is important at the end of the day
Is my family's future when I go away
What sense does it make
If treatment would take
A second mortgage they can never repay?

With no guarantee there's nothing to gain
He'll spend the minimum managing pain
Maggie understands
He's that kind of man
His family comes first for him once again

How will I tell the kids that their dad
The greatest role model they've ever had
Is going to die ?
They're bound to ask why
Mom has no answer, that's what's so sad

Paulie kept working as long as he could
Eventually the painkillers did little good
He tried to stay strong
But it wasn't long
'Til a cripple now lay where a man once stood

Confined to his bed Pauli managed a grin
If one of his friends decided to drop in
The morphine hid well
His personal hell
He tried to be the guy he always had been

Paulie felt it coming some time ahead
Maggie saw it and propped up his head
His kids were there crying
As Paulie was dying
Even the dog was allowed on the bed

Paulie died just where he wanted to be
In his own home with his whole family
Their home is intact
As a matter of fact
Mortgage insurance was so worth the fee

TIME TRAVEL

Jerome is a genius with an IQ off the charts
But he is much more than the sum of his smarts
He has an idea
Which to him is quite clear
But to prove his new theory takes money to start

Gets loans from everyone including the bank
Pawns his belongings on this crazy prank
If his idea works
They'll all feel like jerks
And be the ones to whom he owes his thanks

So he's built a machine for traveling in time
But it has a theoretical limit to its design
No time destination
Before its creation
Can be achieved per the space-time baseline

His plan is quite simple in the initial phase
He'll jump to the future by seventeen days
There pause to consult
The Power Ball result
And in sixteen days prove that genius pays

He starts the machine and he's quickly gone
Forward in time to the date agreed upon
It's a successful jump
With hardly a bump
To check the bodega for the numbers drawn

He got the numbers at the newspaper stand
Then noticed the headline there in his hand
POWER BALL WINNER KILLED
And his heart stood still
News of his death echoed like a brass band

A glimpse of the past and the timeline's intact
But that also infers that he has to go back
'Cause if he should stay
He's no means to pay
The money he borrowed to get things on track

Gina's his only friend back at home
Precocious aged ten she has a crush on Jerome
To the timeline I'll stick it
And give Gina the ticket
They can't squeeze money from my headstone

So in his machine he jumps back to his time
Buys the winning ticket after standing in line
Little Gina's moonstruck
At this stroke of luck
He gives her the ticket with a wink at his crime

Jerome sits at home knowing his time is soon
Gina wins the lottery and she's over the moon
She runs to tell Jerome
But on her way home
She's hit by a car 'cuz the timeline's immune

TRAVELIN' JACK

This story follows the life of one man as he travels the country using only his wits and cunning. It takes place around the time of the Great Depression when there were several hundred thousand itinerant workers roaming the land in search of work and, ultimately, survival. They were called by different names like hobo, vagabond, itinerant worker, etc. They all shared a common bond and were known to leave signs for each other, mostly carved in trees or fence posts, even on the sides of houses, to alert others to the presence of work, danger, dogs, police, etc. This particular hobo is fictional, though representative of those people who fought to scrape a living out of whatever they could find.

> *Our story begins somewhere in the mountains of the eastern United States. Jack and his fellow travelers have seen temperatures falling and know it's time to start heading South. They like the mountains as there is always game to trap and no shortage of fresh water in the cool streams. But, as always, time to move on.*

A cool Autumn morning in the Carolina hills
The sun's just beginning to burn off the chill
More firewood required
To stoke up the fire
I might as well do it, they're layin' in still

Left Foot O'Dell tried to jump a boxcar
And lost his right foot tho' he didn't miss far
Patch Duggan's only got
One eye that ain't shot
And Pickin' Willie lives to play his guitar

Ol' Grumpy John hates everyone he knows
He's pretty much harmless so with us he goes
And there's me, Travelin' Jack
Who follows the track
Just a band of vagabonds in seedy old clothes

We hopped the Norfolk Southern to Alabam'
Left Foot's got a sister in Birmingham
But he says we can't go
She won't give no more dough
Last time he left there he felt the door slam

Pickin' Willie told a tale under the stars
'Bout how he tried sleepin' in a freezer car
They poured ice on his head
He thought sure he was dead
But his crazy ass was saved by that ol' guitar

Us hobos spin yarns late at night by the fire
But Grumpy John up and called Willie a liar
It cost John his life
By way of Willie's knife
Gone to his glory without clergy or choir

A boxcar with straw in the Birmingham yard
We sneak aboard early to throw off the guard
These cars feel like home
But we ain't alone
I meet up with a face all wrinkled and scarred

It's a woman I see and she's black as the night
Runnin' from something by her look of fright
Bustin' in on her comes
Four ragged ol' bums
I'd be scared too, hell we must look a sight

Once she calms down, she tells me her name
Folks call her Annie and the reason she came
Is she's been a slave
Since her fam'ly gave
Her up to some white folks to settle a claim

I tell her we don't mean no harm to no one
Just ridin' the rails from sun to setting sun
She can join us or not
So she casts her lot
With us so we'll help her to stay on the run

As we head West Annie says there's a town
In Mississippi where we might settle down
Tho' that's not our way
For just a few days
Maybe we'll drive a few stakes in the ground

In Biloxi we meet Annie's cousins who live
Off the catfish and shrimp and willing to give
A kind helping hand
And a small piece of land
To use as a campsite 'til we're ready to leave

After a few weeks in the care of Annie's kinfolk, the time to move on has come once again. Hobos never like to stay in one place too long, so it's time to say goodbye.

We been layin' around Biloxi far too long
Left Foot says we should already be gone
Patch Duggan and me
Are wont to agree
And Pickin' Willie's singin' a sad, sad song

Annie and her family are the finest of folks
We even took a turn on the shrimpin' boats
Some work and good food
With our spirits renewed
There's still time to leave on a positive note

One of Annie's cousins, Delroy is his name
Wants to travel with us if we are all game
He's a big so-and-so
Tho' a little bit slow
A big man is handy in scrapes all the same

Along with Delroy Annie rejoins the band
Naturally we don't have anything planned
Anyway, she knows
This crew always goes
Wherever the call of the rails may demand

Weather is pushing us further to the West
The Southern Pacific will have a few guests
Luzyann's the first place
We can claim us a space
Thumbin's gonna be big Delroy's first test

Not many folks will likely help a black man
As luck would have it one came by who can
Black farmers are rare
But here's one who cares
We rode with his chickens right into Luzyann'

Squattin' outside a small town for the night
To head for the rail line next day at first light
But a few men from town
Didn't want us around
All of them drunk and spoilin' for a fight

They went for Delroy as if they had a plan
He killed one of them with just a right hand
The rest piled on him
And pinned ev'ry limb
Then dragged him away to a juniper stand

A rope had appeared before anyone knew
Tied into a noose and when they were thru
Delroy had been hung
At just twenty-one
We must protect Annie or they'll kill her too

Travelin' at night is not how we move along
We take our sweet time answering the song
But now we gotta leave
There's no time to grieve
We have to get moving and try to be strong

Trudging thru the night we arrive at the yard
But the Southern Pacific has the gates barred
Patch says, "Just wait!"
And opens the gate
He can get around locks and security guards

Safe in the boxcar Annie's cryin' in my lap
She feels like she led Delroy into a trap
So can't tell her kin
What happened to him
She's now one of us and she's quick to adapt

Next mornin' the cars are getting ready to go
What they'll put in ours you just never know
It turns out to be hay
For horses on the way
We'll have a soft bed but provisions are low

Now on the move and running from whatever those townsfolk had in mind, the group spends the next few days hiding in the freight car and rationing the precious little they have left to eat. They will hold out as long as they can but will have to stop soon to resupply.

Somewhere in Texas we jumped off the train
Spotting a farmhouse a ways across the plain
It has a large barn
And it can't do no harm
To ask if they'll let us sleep out of the rain

Too many like us would have stealin' in mind
For them it comes natural but I ain't that kind
If you're honest with folks
There's no need to coax
They're gonna help you if they're so inclined

Luckily the farmer needs some more hands
Bringin' in the crop or it rots where it stands
He'll show us good favor
Reward honest labor
With food for our travel, some even canned

We sleep in the barn and work in the fields
The food in the morning holds much appeal
Fresh eggs and corn gruel
A much-needed fuel
Our joy at this breakfast is hard to conceal

The crop is now in and it's time to move on
In parting he says he'll be sorry we're gone
Salt pork and canned roots
Some coffee to boot
We'll carry along when we depart at dawn

We continue West but soon we must turn
The desert only offers a real bad sunburn
A Northwestern route
Is better, no doubt
As Winter recedes the cold is less concern

Annie and I have grown much closer of late
An unlikely pair thrown together by fate
But a mixed-race couple
Is asking for trouble
Back roads and boxcars avoid all the hate

Those of our kind will pay no mind to us
Taking the attitude, "What's all the fuss?"
With shelter to find
And no axe to grind
Better things to do than sit and discuss

Several days have gone by since the farm
Left Foot's the first one to raise the alarm
Of all we brought on
The food's almost gone
All of the salt pork and most of the corn

On top of all this Annie's under the weather
Looking at her I know nothing is better
She pulls me aside
And says, "I'm with child!"
I hug her and say, "We'll do this together."

We gather the others to give them the news
And see if they have the heart to excuse
The shortage is due
To her eating for two
We'll get off now if that's what they choose

Silence for a second then Willie says, "No,
who's gonna play for that child if you go?"
We started to laugh
And I said, "On behalf
of the 3 of us thanks, it ain't easy, I know."

We get off next morning to refill our larder
More now required so it's gonna be harder
The next train comes thru
In a week, maybe two
We hope other bo's have left a few markers

The crew goes about the task of gathering supplies before the next train passes thru. Meanwhile, Annie's baby continues to grow, soon becoming obvious, even underneath her heavy clothing.

The Southern Pacific has saved us again
We're sharin' a car with an older black man
Says he's a preacher
And grade school teacher
Saw his church torched by the KuKluxKlan

It's not hard to believe what he says is true
We've seen in person what the Klan will do
Introductions are made
His name's Virgil Slade
"Folks call me Parson, if it's OK with you."

He's a comfort to Annie, that much is clear
For whatever reason it's good that he's here
We hope the next town
Has a midwife around
She'll have to be black so Parson volunteers

We reckon we're somewhere in Colorado
Not many towns but the train starts to slow
"Should we gamble that here,
on this barren frontier,
we'll find what we need?" No way to know

Annie says soon we won't have to decide
The baby will come when its time's arrived
Since that is the case
This must be the place
All are agreed the child won't be denied

Well shy of the town is just the right time
Without a full moon, conditions are prime
The train slows some more
And we're out the door
Headed for a nearby copse of white pine

At this time in our history black folks usually lived in a separate (and inevitably poorer) part of town referred to as The Bottoms. It's here that Parson is most likely to locate a midwife and sympathy for their situation.

As soon as we've set up a camp with a fire
Parson heads for town so he can inquire
In a neighborly way
Where the black townsfolk stay
The Bottoms is where he'll look to acquire

Gone thru the night he returns at daybreak
A black lady named Georgia trails in his wake
She smiles at them all
And says, "Well y'all
got ya'self a baby but couldn't birth a snake!"

We all bust out laughin' after worryin' so
Parson explains she will help us although
Her place in the town
Is much safer ground
But only Miss Annie and Parson may go

Nobody knows how long this might take
But we must be patient for the baby's sake
Next morning we need
To find us some feed
The rest of us go out in search of a stake

While they wait for word on Annie's baby, Jack, Patch, Willie and Left Foot scour the country nearby and find a friendly farmer who lets them do odd jobs for food. They return to camp each night hoping for news.

One day we wake in the morning to see
Parson and the midwife sitting near a tree
"We got a baby boy!"
Parson's filled with joy
"Georgia guided Annie thru the delivery."

He said all that with a twinkle in his eye
Georgia sitting quietly seems a little shy
He says Annie's fine
The baby shows good sign
Then he tells us the rest with a heavy sigh

We know this life on the rails ain't his way
And the people here have asked him to stay
They don't have a preacher
Or even a teacher
To educate the children or teach 'em to pray

An old church here could double as a school
To teach readin', writin' and the golden rule
But Georgia is why
There's stars in his eyes
Parson is actin' like a lovesick old fool

The folks of The Bottoms, poor tho' they be
Packed up some goods for the new family
Bacon and fatback
Salt pork and hardtack
Canned fruit, green beans and a jar of honey

Canning, or 'putting up', is a process of storing food when abundant in anticipation of leaner times. Ironically, glass jars with rubber seals for the lids, are used instead of cans and many people still can today.

Annie and the baby will be joining us soon
The next train will be here tomorrow at noon
It's risky during the day
But we can't have our way
Our journey's delayed and it's time to resume

At night Annie comes with the baby in tow
She's smiling brightly and can't wait to show
The small new addition
To our travelin' mission
Patch asks his name but we don't yet know

Annie says Jasper is Georgia's older brother
He is the one who kept things under cover
Brought supplies late at night
To keep us out of sight
Did everything needed to protect the new mother

The baby's now Jasper and we're all satisfied
But before we can sleep a problem to decide
Is how to board the train
'Cuz if it doesn't rain
Anyone could spot us catchin' a free ride

Parson volunteers to provide a distraction
By carryin' a sigh he'll be the main attraction
Askin' for donations
To his black congregation
He's bound to receive one hell of a reaction

The train pulls in as its brakes loudly hiss
A crowd of white folks is gathered for this
But when Parson arrives
They all run for their lives
Jumping on quickly we blow Parson a kiss

With their number increased by one they continue Northwestward thru Colorado and on to the Pacific coast. Now that the weather has warmed sufficiently, they are not so bothered by the higher altitude.

Our camp is not far from the railroad track
We've got rabbit stew on the cookin' rack
Our bedding is laid
But where has Patch strayed?
He went to fetch water, why isn't he back?

Water is life so we've camped near a creek
It's fed by a snow-covered mountain peak
But something is wrong
He's been gone far too long
Now from the woods we hear a loud shriek

I jump to my feet as Annie runs to my side
Nature had called and of course she replied
"Our poor Patch is dead
and he's torn to shreds!"
She's crying and shaking and fit to be tied

She quiets a bit and points back at the trees
With Willie behind me I go have a look see
Sure enough he's there
And been mauled by a bear
Or cougar perhaps, same difference to me

This place isn't safe if that beast is around
We must get out now before we are found
With no train to be caught
Can't have second thoughts
We follow the track Northwesterly bound

It ain't the first time we've walked the track
But none here ever had a baby on his back
We all share the load
So our pace won't be slowed
Still in my mind is how Patch was attacked

We walk thru the night and into the next day
Tired as we are there ain't nowhere to stay
But Left Foot spots smoke
Could be a lucky stroke
It's ahead in the woods and still far away

We keep to the track and watch for a sign
They'll see us first up here walkin' the line
We're nearin' the spot
When we hear a shot
And a figure walks into the bright sunshine

It's a man with a rifle and a hat pulled low
Blocking the track so we've nowhere to go
We stop and stand still
Hoping we don't get killed
Then he walks toward us movin' real slow

He stops and slings the rifle over his back
Lookin' at me asks, "That be you, Jack?"
Music to my ears
After all these years
"In the flesh, Billy", I quickly answer back

Billy Red Cloud spent a lifetime on the rails
Hoppin' town to town when he wasn't in jail
A full-blooded Chinook
He never once took
Abuse from a white man, or ever turned tail

His hobo days over, he's finally settled down
Returned to his people on this tribal ground
The gathering is small
And we're welcomed by all
Food and spring water are passed all around

Billy is wondering if we've made any plans
He is sure to recall how we traveled the land
Cross the Northern Plains
Stay ahead of the rains
Farmers always looking for temporary hands

Has Billy again run afoul of the law?
His temper was always a character flaw
But he's just thinking back
To our days on the track
He's satisfied to stay right here with his squaw

Billy has noticed how Left Foot's behavin'
He' taken a shine to one of the maidens
Although she's not young
She still has no son
Maybe Left Foot is what she's been cravin'

He's traveled so far on crutches he made
And the light in his eyes is beginning to fade
This life takes its toll
On body and soul
It will always catch up and can't be delayed

Soon we will head for the Northern farm belt
Left Foot will remain and his loss will be felt
His decision is smart
To follow his heart
We all play our hand with what we were dealt

Billy and his people have prepared a big feast
To bid us farewell on our journey to the East
We wait near the track
For that clickety-clack
Left Foot remains and I hope he finds peace

The Southern Pacific is on time once again
With a wave we are gone and soon settle in
This time we're alone
Four souls on our own
As the train steams East, a new journey begins

They work their way East through the farms of the Plains, having timed their arrival as the crops are ready for harvest. They have little use for money, rather work for food, shelter and enough provisions to reach the next stop.

Now that the Northern Plains are left behind
We've made our way to the West Virginia line
There's food in our kit
So we'll just rest a bit
Jasper's now walking and that's a good sign

We bypassed the cities of Ohio and Illinois
They're way too crowded to find any joy
You can't breathe the air
We'd suffocate there
And they'd never tolerate our half-breed boy

The air in the country is clean as can be
Our way of living is what it means to be free
Jasper runnin' around
Willie sleepin' sound
On a blanket of soft grass lay Annie and me

We've been thru here many times in the past
These folks let us camp without bein' asked
Some are moonshiners
Most are coal miners
And couldn't care less that we are outcasts

We'll take our own time travelin' thru the hills
And linger until we feel Winter's first chill
We depend on the seasons
To show us the reasons
It's time to move on and we certainly will

Jack and company have circled the country in the course of a year, depending on the weather to guide them. They will continue this for many years 'til Jasper is grown and they are back in these hills once again.

Our boy is a gangling young man of eighteen
In spite of the life he has grown tall and lean
Curly hair and dark skin
Where can he fit in?
Half-breeds like him are called in-betweens

I've taught him all I can, he's now on his own
Annie and I are proud of how he's grown
When he leaves we can't go
Life has taken its toll
How much longer we have, nobody knows

Willie wants badly to go back on the road
But it's easy to see how his walk has slowed
Jasper says he'll stay
And oh, by the way
He tells us he thinks an explanation is owed

Seems there's this girl he's met recently
Like Annie a slave but is now walking free
Her owner has granted
Some land to be planted
A reparation for her unrighteous slavery

First, they'll build a cabin as Winter is near
It has to be quickly if they wish to stay here
They begin to cut trees
Before there's a freeze
But whether they'll make it is not at all clear

The weather is brutal and progress is slow
They have little shelter and nowhere to go
Soon Annie takes ill
With fever and chills
Her death in the morning is a terrible blow

Jack is left to wonder what sense it all makes
She'd still be alive if they'd pulled up stakes
He's got the rail fever
But he cannot leave her
He must try to live with this awful heartache

The cabin is finished and planting is done
Jasper is waiting for the preacher to come
Marryin's in style
When the bride is with child
And Willie decided to go back on the run

Each morning he took fresh flowers to her grave
Sat down and thanked her for the love she gave
When he didn't come back
They went looking for Jack
Who was now reunited with his Annie, the slave

TRUE LOVE

Our kids are ugly and you're the reason
The smell of your breath is really displeasin'
You've moles on your face
And it's not the only place
Your body hair often sets me to sneezin'

You shave every day to control your beard
And the herpes is back just as I feared
Yellow toenails
Skin rough like scales
The acne was treated but still hasn't cleared

The first time we did it I got a bad rash
Down below my waist and all over my ass
You sweat so much
Whenever we touch
And the dog runs for cover when you pass gas

You brought your dear mother to live with us
No matter how I try she still raises a fuss
Calls me bad names
Says I'm to blame
For the ills of the world, I'm a miserable cuss

None of my friends come to visit when asked
We used to be buddies but that's in the past
They can't bear to see
What's happened to me
As long as I'm with you I'll be an outcast

But there are good reasons I must disagree
You love to drink beer and go fishin' with me
No woman good lookin'
Could match your home cookin'
Without you my darlin' oh where would I be?

TURTLES AND TRAINS

When I was a boy I would sit out back
And wait for the train to roll down the track
As it rumbled by
I'd wave a big, "Hi!"
And listen to the sound of the clickety-clack

Most folks around here had horses and cows,
Chickens and pigs with a huge mama sow
They kept 'em fenced in
Like it's always been
Stringing barbed wire on posts, that was how

In summer I'd walk by the track for miles
Chat with a neighbor when I'd rest for a while
There's not much to see
Which was fine with me
Walking and whistling was my fav'rite lifestyle

One day when I'd walked seven miles at most
Something caught my eye atop a fence post
A turtle there sat
Now, how about that
The weather was hot, so hot he might roast

At first I thought, "How did he get up there?"
Turtles can't climb, at least I'm not aware
Guess someone put him
Up there on a whim
Or as a result of a double-dog dare

The top of the post is six feet above ground
Deciding to jump would hardly be sound
What if he landed
So he'd be stranded
Flat on his back with his legs thrashing 'round?

I decided to come to his rescue
My conscience said it's the right thing to do
So I laid him down
Gently on the ground
Preparing to walk on when I was through

But that little guy had other plans for me
Bit down on my shoe so I couldn't flee
And when I looked down
He was wearing a frown
Then he let go and got down on one knee

"Hey, why did you take me off of my spot?"
All I could think of to reply was, "What?"
He's talking to me
A turtle, you see
I know what you're thinking, turtles cannot

I asked him why he was sitting up there
A good explanation seemed only fair
"Since you seem sincere,
I'll try to be clear;
I'm waiting for the train, so why do you care?"

"I thought it was someone's idea of a joke
leaving a turtle in the sun 'til he croaked."
He thought for a sec
Then said, "What the heck?
I guess, after all, you're not a bad bloke."

So I decided to wait for the train
I might never see my new friend again
We talked while we sat
Of this thing and that
'Til we heard the train whistle's sweet refrain

It pulled to a stop right there where we stood
A surprise to me, I didn't think it would
The conductor came down
He reached to the ground
And picked up the turtle, careful as he could

He greeted the turtle, Horace by name
"Good to see you again, so glad you came."
It's a weekly sojourn
I would later learn
He goes to see his girlfriend, a sultry dame

For many years after that I would go
Those seven miles on a Friday although
When he married that dame
He no longer came
To make the journey and I miss him so

TWO FEATHERS

This story was written around a central figure in the style of historical fiction. Although Two Feathers is a product of imagination, the circumstances under which he finds himself are real and every effort was made to portray them accurately.

The deer was alerted right from the start
Its nose in the air and ears far apart
The wind gives no hint
So it can't find his scent
And the hunter's arrow pierces its heart

The carcass lays across his horse's back
As the hunter returns on a well-worn track
His lodge will eat well
But wisdom compels
They salt much away on which to fall back

Two Feathers hasn't taken a wife although
He's now of an age when most make it so
But he has concerns
Of things he has learned
Trees are being cleared so cotton can grow

White men continue to arrive and expand
With little regard for creatures of the land
And none for us, too
The Cherokee who
Wish only peace but are now being banned

They promise us land out in the far West
A wonderful place and we should feel blest
If the land is so fair
Why don't they live there?
And leave us here where our ancestors rest

A treaty called The Indian Removal Act
Was signed into law and is now a fact
It grants power to
The President who
Can now send his army in to attack

Orders come down from the President
All remaining Cherokee are to be sent
To the Reservation
Without hesitation
Their land to be used for white settlement

So the Tribal Council is meeting tonight
Two Feathers says we must stay and fight
No Cherokee runs
Not even from guns
Any who does should be banished from sight

The Council agrees when it solemnly meets
Two Feathers is sent and told what to repeat
His mother implores
"We honor your cause
but so many soldiers you cannot defeat."

Two Feathers returns with the soldiers' reply
"They say we must leave; to remain is to die."
The Council holds firm
Though some seem to squirm
How will we suffer if we fail to comply?

Soldiers arrive to enforce the new law
Riding his horse comes the brave Eagle Claw
Refusing to go
He draws his long bow
Smoke from a rifle was the last thing he saw

The tribe sees Eagle Claw fall to the ground
Right away the women folk gather around
But they cannot save
The Cherokee brave
Now some wonder if the decision was sound

Eagle Claw's killing is a shock to the tribe
The effect on morale is hard to describe
Overwhelming forces
Take wagons and horses
And push the tribe onto a trail they prescribe

Although unwillingly the trek has begun
No choice remains if there's nowhere to run
Many have to walk
Yet still there is talk
Of attempting escape before the next sun

They stop on the first day after sunset
With little to eat, take what you can get
Most sleep on the ground
Where shelter is found
But sometimes the ground is soaking wet

As the days wear on more travelers die
Left where they've fallen with only a sigh
But death takes a toll
On everyone's soul
Even some soldiers have been seen to cry

As the weather grows colder more fall away
And their number grows smaller every day
Both parents now gone
Two Feathers plods on
Vowing that he will make the white man pay

A Cherokee boy who once worked at a fort
Was thrown in this caravan as a last resort.
The army's been cowed
Is no longer allowed
To keep Indian slaves says the military court

Two Feathers located the Cherokee brave
Who picked up English when he was a slave
Each day as they walked
The two of them talked
Searching for a way to escape this enclave

He learns that at night the guards can be few
The days are long, soldiers must sleep too
One person just might
In the cold dead of night
Make their getaway before anyone knew

So there came a night when no moon arose
He knew the young brave wouldn't oppose
He planned to break free
But was warned carefully
They surely will chase him wherever he goes

Wary but not sure how long he can last
Two Feathers decides he can't let this pass
When all's still and damp
He sneaks out of camp
And spots a guard fast asleep on the grass

He silently leads the soldier's horse away
Once out of hearing he jumps on the bay
He'll ride 'til first light
Then hide until night
Missing him takes time so he'll use the delay

For several days he moves through the hills
Grazing the horse and eating what he kills
Though well he has plotted
Soon enough he's spotted
By an Army patrol whose tracker is skilled

They wanted to kill him there on the spot
The commanding officer says they cannot
An example is made
That will surely dissuade
Others from conjuring a similar plot

And so they beat him until he can't stand
Dragging him back to camp by his hands
Tied behind a horse
And pulled with great force
Through briar and bush and mud and sand

For months they push on thru wind and cold
Punishing their bodies, spirits and souls
Until they arrive
Just barely alive
In Oklahoma Territory as was foretold

Two Feathers lost half of his body weight
It's all he can do just to stand up straight
But his sunken eyes
And diminished size
Can't put out the fire that inflames his hate

The tribe can do nothing but make the best
Of this unfamiliar land out here in the West
Their spirits are broken
The white man has spoken
He has no regard for those he's oppressed

Their trek will be known as The Trail of Tears
And read in history books in the coming years
When Two Feathers died
No white settler cried
He took the new land as Two Feathers feared

VICTORY GARDENS

The first world war that America fought
Provided a lesson most brutally taught
To stay on their feet
GI's had to eat
So produce at home could scarcely be bought

We all know soon after the second war came
A fight on two fronts and two enemies to blame
More men to feed
And so to succeed
A plan was developed to wage the campaign

In America the call went out loud and clear
Our soldiers need food that is harvested here
So please grow your own
And reap what is sown
Help the war effort, be a food volunteer

Business and government pitched in as one
Pamphlets were printed and commercials done
Showing folks how
To till, plant and plow
Soon rooftops had gardens up close to the sun

Victory Gardens they were known as back then
When most productive they're said to have been
Equal in yields
To commercial fields
Thus lowering the cost to feed our brave men

Citizens responded and each did his share
Most folks knew someone who fought over there
With shovel and hoe
They made their food grow
To show just how much we Americans care

WEIGHT LOSS

When science probes into the tiniest things
They use two giant accelerator rings
Particles ballistic
At relativistic
Velocities collide and the detectors ping

Exotic new particles are created each day
Most live a short time and then they decay
But some do live on
And once they are gone
Where they end up no one's able to say

The smartest people in the world work here
To them the future of our world was clear
After much brainstorming
About global warming
The LHC team shifted into high gear

Several years later at the Fat Bodies Gym
They're drinking kale juice with satisfied grins
Toasting each other
They've just discovered
Their weight loss total is the best it's been

The moon is each year getting further away
A tiny amount due to reciprocal tide sway
But now it is faster
A potential disaster
What could be causing our satellite to stray?

Global temperatures have started to fall
Only by a bit but it's obvious to all
Fewer hurricanes
More seasonal rains
The animals fatten and the corn grows tall

Measuring the distance from here to the sun
Has proved to be something not easily done
Results not precise
But like the drift ice
We've shifted away when the numbers are run

It's known to scientists that the Earth's core
Is a spinning sphere of molten iron ore
Our magnetic field
The primary shield
From solar radiation is smaller than before

Scientists at CERN had discovered a way
To stall some particles' imminent decay
Then guided them down
Deep underground
Into the Earth's core but they didn't stay

They started a miniature nuclear reaction
But scientists held it to a very small fraction
Mass was converted
Then energy diverted
Into the soil in a heated transaction

As total mass decreased its gravitation fell
The effect on the moon would very soon tell
When the time was right
They shut it down tight
Earth was now farther from the sun as well

But CERN wanted all in the world to know
This couldn't be repeated and told us so
If we move further out
Then without any doubt
We'll collide with Mars in one fiery blow

So we have one last opportunity to clean
Our factories and other polluting machines
Gravitation receded
Less energy needed
Let's all make this planet pristine once again

WENDELL SYKES

The year's twenty thirty and automation
Has gained a foothold across the nation
There are jobs being lost
At a high human cost
Unfeeling robots taking over workstations

Wendell Sykes is a welding fabricator
From an Illinois company in South Decatur
Devout family man
On a union plan
Three kids who can clean out a refrigerator

The foreman brings Wendell a hot new design
He's their go to guy when a lot's on the line
The best on the crew
He's always come through
For thirty-five years come rain or come shine

What is the function of this new machine?
Tolerances more precise than he's ever seen
Aluminum and steel
To weld and anneal
This job will require lots of acetylene

Wendell starts in by cutting pieces to size
How many there are is a bit of a surprise
His vigor's undiminished
Perhaps when he's finished
The thing will make sense, but not as it lies

It's finally done but it seems incomplete
Standing upright on six aluminum feet
An odd-looking rack
With hooks in the back
But it's just like the plan, satisfaction is sweet

Next day the foreman meets him at the door
Seems his services aren't required anymore
His final project
Replaced him in effect
It holds robotic welders like none seen before

The only job available was working in a bar
Reflecting on how he could have fallen so far
No college for the kids
Because of what he did
No gold watch was given or box of cigars

One night at the bar the foreman came by
And ordered a beer in which he could cry
He's out of work too
'Cuz nothing to do
The factory's automated, no one need apply

This story is fictionally sad but it's true
No matter your skills it could happen to you
What jobs will remain
In the robots' domain?
Few with high wages if retraining won't do

WHISTLING RILL

Not nearly a river but more than a creek
Snowmelt and rain from the mountain peak
Flowing down the hill
Carve out a wide rill
Creating the splendor of which I now speak

In Springtime the water runs especially fast
It makes a whistling sound as it rushes past
The smooth granite rocks
And many outcrops
Makes a soft lullaby as the last light is cast

Life in the mountains requires many skills
You have to be able to hunt, trap and kill
Clear water's a must
Or else you go bust
So we built our cabin next to Whistling Rill

The water is clear and sweet as you please
Corn grows tall and we give it a squeeze
Then cook it a while
Mountain country style
But keeping the still hidden deep in the trees

One year there came a massive snowfall
Much more than anyone here could recall
It would have been harder
Without a full larder
'Cuz hunting was paltry that year in the Fall

When the Spring arrived it all began to melt
That was the hardest blow we'd been dealt
The water was rising
Which wasn't surprising
But so quickly the danger was easily felt

Before long the water was at the cabin door
The cabin was safe with just a dirt floor
But we were in danger
And death was no stranger
So we sought higher ground as never before

'Twas a month and then some before our return
Our cabin was fine but we had some concern
The bed of the rill
Was cut deeper still
A consequence of which we had yet to learn

Our little boy played in the rill every day
Looking for tadpoles that might swim his way
And collecting the stones
That sparkled and shone
To spread out and admire in a rocky array

Little boys leave things in pockets all the time
Forgetful of all as they run, jump and climb
And so Mom discovered
What he had uncovered
When washing his pants to get out the grime

The stones she found in his pockets were gold
Nuggets they were, if the truth would be told
Much more gold was found
In the uncovered ground
But this was a threat to our beloved freehold

The gold would be hidden and never talked of
A rush to these parts would kill all that we love
Our son can stay on
Once we are gone
Or use all that gold to make a new life thereof

WHO AM I

Walking in the dark I seek out a streetlight
Pajamas and bathrobe, I must look a sight
How I got here
Is not really clear
My memory is cloudy this time of night

I see a policeman out walking his beat
His face looks familiar so I cross the street
I offer my hand
"Do you know who I am?"
He smiles knowingly as he stares at my feet

With only my slippers to keep out the cold
I can't fight it off now that I've gotten old
And it's getting colder
But his hand's on my shoulder
He leads me back home without being told

The doctors say I shouldn't be out on my own
My dementia, they say, is nearly full blown
But what do they know?
I still get up and go
So what if I can't always find my way home?

They're not giving up and want me to stay
Keep insisting the court can make me obey
But when I've sundowned
They've no legal grounds
'Cuz I'm not accountable for anything I say

When I am lucid I won't give consent
No bed for me behind walls of cement
I'll never be stored
In the Alzheimer ward
It isn't a hospital but an old tenement

I know I'm still out there even if I can't see
What good is a life that isn't lived free?
My memory's fine
Most of the time
But when I forget I'll go looking for me

We all will grow old
But not the same way
For some life turns gold
While others see grey

WILD HORSES

The Big Sky country of the Western Plains
Hosts balmy summers and seasonal rains
In Winter it snows
And freezing wind blows
But the azure skies return again and again

On a high plateau The Wellness Center lies
Seems a healthy retreat to the untrained eye
But palliative care's
The specialty there
In truth it's a place where the rich go to die

During Winter Clarissa arrived on the scene
She bequeathed a fortune as well as a gene
Though dormant it lies
Is destined to rise
To shut down the work of the body's machine

Born in the deep South on a huge plantation
The cold and the snow not her ideal vacation
Didn't know how to ski
Or drive a Cat-V
The ride on the snowmobile too much vibration

Days spent reading by the warmth of the fire
'Til sleep overtook and time came to retire
The days dawdled by
Watching the white sky
Until the sun returned to melt the quagmire

Four-wheel drive vehicles are available to all
The first warm day she dons scarf and shawl
Driving off to explore
The valley and more
Reluctantly returning just prior to nightfall

This is horse country and one day she found
A herd of wild horses far from the compound
Their leader appeared
Snorted and reared
Then cautiously approached, head held down

He came near and looked Clarissa in the eye
Turned and walked away, his head held high
Upon rejoining the herd
Their interest stirred
He led them away to graze quietly nearby

She was used to horses behaving this way
Clarissa rode on the plantation every day
The locals who worked
At the center all smirked
Wild horses would have stayed very far away

Soon Clarissa was walking among the herd
Stroking and speaking soft comforting words
But she couldn't explain
Her deep hidden pain
The death gene inside her had started to stir

Did she see a sadness in the stallion's eyes?
Can the horses detect her imminent demise?
Very soon she must stay
In her deathbed all day
Her sorrow at missing them hard to disguise

At last Clarissa lost her battle with the gene
The staff at the center marveled at the scene
Outside the glass door
Heads low to the floor
The herd of wild horses stood still and serene

WILLA

Her mother had boyfriends all over town
But policy was not to bring them around
Best they stay away
Lest a hungry eye stray
Young Willa at home was forbidden ground

This one was different or so she had thought
She relished the gifts and liquor he bought
And so when she drank
More reason to thank
The man with the money she eagerly sought

Drunk at their wedding did she even recall
Him clinging to Willa at the reception hall?
The look on his face
Was way out of place
Far better to let sleeping dogs lie after all

It started when Willa was thirteen years old
Her stepfather getting more and more bold
A slap on the rear
And calling her Dear
She too naive to know what this foretold

He began to enter her room late at night
She tried to struggle and put up a fight
But he was too strong
And so before long
It was all over and he grinned with delight

Her mother was always in an alcoholic daze
Oblivious to all and so nothing could faze
Was her mother aware?
Did she even care?
She didn't try to stop the man's brutal ways

When barely sixteen Willa finally broke free
Slipped out at night when no one would see
She ran 'til past dawn
Making sure she's long gone
"When he wakes up he'll be looking for me."

Begging for food Willa lived on the street
Bone chilling cold and fierce summer heat
Odd jobs time to time
For nickels and dimes
Struggling so hard just to stay on her feet

For years Willa did what she had to do
But selling her body was strictly taboo
She hoped for a man
Who could understand
Her past and the misery she'd been put thru

Butch was a fry cook at Burgers and Buns
A place where young people go to have fun
Car hops on skates
Serve french fries and shakes
He gave food to Willa when his shift was done

They'd sit by the curb and talk while they ate
She found herself thinking, "Is this like a date?"
The feelings she had
Sure didn't feel bad
But if it's not real then she'd just have to wait

He seemed like a guy who knew love from lust
Maybe it's time that she started to trust
"If he'll take it slow
we might give it a go.
This life can't continue so it looks like I must."

Butch has an old car he's finally paid off
It usually runs but it sputters and coughs
Sometimes it stalls
And the tires are bald
It once had a spare but it must have been lost

His apartment is a double bed and a sink
A hotplate and dishes that have missing chinks
Down a narrow hall
A bathroom that's small
He's started to wonder what Willa might think

If a cardboard box is your only bed
Any place softer to lay down your head
Is a welcome change
And so they arranged
That Willa would join his modest homestead

Her first time with Butch was so different than
The pain she endured with that horrible man
His soft, gentle touch
Aroused her so much
She clung to him tightly as the feelings began

Soon she felt new life beginning inside
Butch was a new man beaming with pride
He worked late at night
His dream now in sight
Something to stive for had now been supplied

The baby's kick puts a smile on her face
After years of sadness, this happy place
The journey was long
But he kept her strong
Believing in him was her saving grace

Tonight he is late which he never has been
Willa is worried when she sees the two men
They knock on her door
There's bad news in store
The policemen tell her what happened to him

A reckless drunk driver hit him broadside
Traveling so fast Butch instantly died
When they pulled him out
There was little doubt
It happened so fast that all pain was denied

She prayed to her god as she fell to the ground
But when gods are needed, they aren't around
They insist that you pray
And mindlessly obey
But you're left all alone when the chips are down

As she cries on the floor a bolt of sharp pain
Shoots through her body again and again
There's blood on her shirt
"My baby is hurt!"
How she got to the hospital she can't explain

A nurse comes to check if Willa is awake
There's more bad news that she has to break
Her face is forlorn
The baby's stillborn
Abandoned again to endure this heartache

Back on the street drugs have taken her down
If this is her life then why hang around?
Her mother escaped
The monster who raped
Her Willa who's being consigned to the ground

ZERO POINT ENERGY

Imagine that space is constructed of fields
And each point within it potentially yields
An energy source
Of formidable force
If humans could harness the power it wields

Quantum mechanics seems magical at best
But tries to explain why nothing's at rest
Make everything freeze
As cold as you please
Vibrations still occur and can't be suppressed

A minimum energy's always required
No matter the system or how it is wired
We don't see a trace
In the vacuum of space
But the ripples exist to be used as desired

Ten times the power of our nuclear fission
Available everywhere for acquisition
No more fossil fuels
Or environmental duels
Finally ending all that carbon emission

So what if researchers really did find a way
To use this new bounty in homes every day?
Gasoline is conceded
Electricity not needed
What would become of big industry's sway?

Trillions of dollars of loss would ensue
For Exxon and ConEd this just wouldn't do
They'd wrap it up tight
To never see the light
So maybe this dream has already come true!

ZOMBIES

Creatures not alive but they aren't dead
Wander about with no thought in their heads
A blank lifeless stare
From eyes unaware
Social media appetites craving to be fed

The world goes by but they couldn't care less
Never doing anything leaves naught to confess
Their eyes glued to screens
On handheld machines
A disappearing signal their only distress

No human contact required for this lot
Social skill development never got a shot
Texting not talking
A life of sleepwalking
Turning into zombies as their brains slowly rot

An entire generation is lost in cyberspace
Never fit in 'cause they haven't a place
A future unsure
Will they even endure
Or just delete themselves, leaving no trace?

POCKET OF TIME

When we gaze at the night sky we see trillions of stars, billions of galaxies, planets, moons and even the occasional comet. If we bring our large telescopes to bear there are many more objects visible, some of them quite strange. But all these phenomena have one thing in common...they are not unique. If you find one black hole you are sure to find thousands more. Even the rarest of these, like the magnetar, has cousins lurking elsewhere. So we must ask the question, "Is anything in the universe unique, truly one of a kind?" I know of one occurrence so rare that, as far as I know, is the only one to ever exist. At least I have never heard of another and I read the scientific journals now and again. In any event, it happened and that is what my story is about.

The Rift

Thousands of years ago something caused the fabric of spacetime to split and when it did one side of the resulting rift folded under itself, then around and back to form a huge new pocket of spacetime. The rift then closed leaving the pocket, along with everything residing in the affected space in a dimension of sorts, separate from the rest of spacetime. This event occurred near an ocean and there was an island present at the time. The island, approximately the size of Colorado, and its inhabitants were now living in the new pocket of spacetime.

As strange as this all seems, it is far stranger yet, as time did not move in the newly formed pocket as it does in the surrounding spacetime. The estimate of when this happened is not very accurate but, supposing it happened about 3,000 years ago, the time in the new pocket would have advanced more than 5,000 years (fortunately, time in the pocket moves in the same direction). The inhabitants of the island would therefore be far more advanced than their counterparts in this spacetime.

To make things easier I will refer to the spacetime in the pocket as In-Pocket and the rest of spacetime as Out-Of-Pocket. The In-Pocket inhabitants, having lived on an island all this time, would necessarily develop their civilization in an entirely different manner than Out-Of-Pocket peoples. It is not known whether these people had established contact or trade with other islands or a mainland based on artifacts left from the time of the rift. As mentioned, the rift closed when the pocket formed but it did not, and does not to this day, remain closed.

In-Pocket People

We all are products of our environment and the In-Pocket people are no exception. When a population reaches the point where the land it inhabits can no longer sustain it one of two things must occur; it either vanishes or adapts. This is particularly true for an island nation and the residents were quick to modify their habits and were eventually vindicated for it.

The first and most pressing issue was population control.

It was agreed that many should first die in the normal course of things before any births could occur. After a time the population had decreased naturally and a new problem arose. With all those burials came a realization that land was too precious for this kind of wasted space. Since they obtained a good portion of their sustenance from the sea, it seemed only fitting to return the favor by committing the bodies of the dead to a watery grave, thus providing nutrition to the creatures therein. These at-sea burials would evolve into solemn family services honoring both the dead and the sea that provided them so much.

As time passed it became clear that each citizen relied heavily on every other one, not only in day-to-day life but in the special ability that each possessed and brought to bear in providing all that was needed to survive. They had already developed strong family ties and this led to family specialization and family businesses. But they had never had need for what would in the Out-Of-Pocket world be called money. Rather, each contributed to the economy and in turn took what he needed; there was never any question that someone would take more than required. Throughout the land there were stalls where food and other staples were kept, never locked away, so any who wished could take what was needed. When a fishing boat returned it was not uncommon for a crowd to gather at the dock to applaud the captain and crew, thus thanking them for their catch. The same was true when a farmer brought his crop to market or an engineering family announced a new design of one or another of the things people used.

In this way each's appreciation of all others was reaffirmed and solidified. Families who studied the science of the human body eventually removed all disease from their civilization. Faster and larger fishing vessels and soon enough flying machines were invented. This last would finally allow the In-Pocket people to discover, much to their dismay, the limits of the world they had come to love.

Discovery

As mentioned earlier, time moved differently In-Pocket and while the Out-Of-Pocket world passed through the Industrial Revolution the In-Pocket world had far outstripped their progress.

They had mastered gravity and fusion energy to the point that every home was powered individually as were the small vehicles that dotted the landscape. These were used as "ground-based" transportation although they did not sit on the ground, only close enough so that passengers could get on and off. The island had long ago been mapped and all were familiar with it although buildings might go up or down at any time. Land was not allocated so the only restriction on someone who wanted to build was that it did not interfere with another's space. Thus, there were no streets; in fact, the people themselves were the only things with names. Anyone could jump in one of these small "taxis" and point out his destination on the holographic map which appeared and he was off.

If the taxi was required to pass over a building it simply did so and the occupant(s) would not feel any sense of movement. Taxis came in all sizes, from a one-person scooter vehicle to a large bus-like affair that could hold many passengers. If truth be known, people would often take these around the island just for fun since fuel was inexhaustible.

But the most advanced vehicles were the flying machines. These could reach tremendous velocities and make instant turns without the pilot feeling any sense of movement or centrifugal force. They were self-contained and could navigate through water as easily as through air. It was in one of these that one man decided to see how far he could go from home one day. Shooting straight off toward the horizon at a high rate of speed he intended to look for other islands like his own.

After some time, he reached a shoreline but soon realized he had come right back where he started. "How could this be?", he wondered. When others were alerted to this seemingly impossible circumstance an effort was mounted to attempt to map the entirety of their world. After many months the Pocket had been mapped and the people realized that, large as their world was, they could never leave it. Their world was confined, both horizontally and vertically; travel outside was impossible in any direction. A curious people who looked to the stars finally realized they would never dance among them.

The Rift Opens

One day a fishing vessel was plying the sea far from home when it came across a small craft that appeared to be some sort of primitive boat. The crew drew near enough to see inside and found that all aboard had died, seemingly of old age. The mainland was alerted and soon the sky was abuzz with all manner of flying machines. Soon other seafaring vessels had joined the montage but none had an explanation for this odd little craft. Since the crew were dead, they were consigned to the sea as was the In-Pocket custom. The little boat was scuttled as its material was of no use to them.

That would have been the end of it had not one of the flying machines noticed a peculiar shimmering light off in the distance. Upon investigation it was clear he had found a passageway into another world! This was known to be the edge of their world as mapped earlier and the pilot could not resist flying through it. He darted about this new world for a short time but feared that this opening might close at any moment and he would not be able to return home.

And so back he went to report this wondrous discovery to his fellows. The news caused an understandable excitement among the inhabitants and the scientific families were called upon to investigate the phenomena thoroughly. By the time they arrived the shimmering light was gone but they were able to detect residual shifts in the magnetic fields and there were certain time anomalies as well. These were all studied on scene for some time until they detected growing changes in the magnetic field once again.

Soon the shimmering space returned and the doorway to the outside world reopened. The scientists felt sure that they could now predict the opening and closing of "The Rift" based upon the initial changes that preceded an opening or closing. Soon flyers were equipped with these measuring devices and pilots began exploring the Out-Of-Pocket world in earnest. As soon as their instruments warned of an imminent closing of the Rift they would scurry back home, none wishing to be trapped in an alien environment. While they could predict an opening and closing just prior to the event, as far as they could tell the frequency of these occurrences was completely random.

The Out-Of-Pocket World

Flyers continued to traverse in and out of the Out-Of-Pocket world for many years and the tales they brought back were of war, crime, starvation and political corruption. But they also returned with data that showed that In-Pocket people aged much more slowly than normal while they were in the Out-Of-Pocket spacetime. This is what led them to measure time in both and finally explained the dead people they had encountered years ago in the small sailing craft.

It meant that, conversely, Out-Of-Pocket people aged far more quickly while In-Pocket. Those unfortunate sailors were Out-Of-Pocket residents who had inadvertently sailed through the Rift. Apparently, they were no more aware of it than the In-Pocket people. The unanswered question remains, "Why didn't the original inhabitants age quickly and die when the Rift occurred?"

Nevertheless, while Out-Of-Pocket people could not survive In-Pocket for more than a few hours, the In-Pocket people, who could live far longer Out-Of-Pocket, had no desire to do so after hearing the stories told by returning flyer pilots. Well, almost none.

Confession

If you've stayed with me this far you are surely questioning everything I've said and likely don't believe a word of it. I have proof, however, if you will bear with me a bit longer. You folks have been watching those flyers for many years without realizing it. You've called them flying saucers, UFO's and several other acronyms, the latest being UAP; curious, this penchant you have for acronyms. You've also seen and experienced the Rift. If you chanced to fly over it while it was open you would have seen a shimmering light in the waves below and undoubtedly would have just considered it reflections off the water. But you have encountered it as well; your vessels have sailed near it when it was open and their navigation and compasses were rendered useless. Some planes have even fallen in to the rift as a result, to sink in the sea, their pilots dying quickly of old age. You call this area the Bermuda Triangle.

So how do I know all this? I was born In-Pocket but have been living in your world since my flyer crashed many years ago in a place called Roswell (by the way, that story about finding an alien body at the crash site was baloney). I could have returned In-Pocket but I am a curious sort and hope to live long enough to watch you all blow yourselves to hell.

The End

THE LINGA WARS

Long before the elves arrived the fairies had mastered both the earth and the sky. Their large gossamer wings allowed them to soar above their forest home and float on the breeze. They built their homes of wood and earth throughout the forest that they shared with countless other creatures and lived a peaceful coexistence with them all. The fairies had voices but they didn't speak, rather communicated with each other using pictures, of a sort, that they exchanged with their minds. These pictures could convey much more than the intended thought or idea; those who received the picture could also sense the mood, state of mind, and importance of the message to the sender. In most cases, the animals and birds which shared their home were able to receive these pictures as well. In many instances, the fairies could read pictures from the minds of some of them, even though they could not consciously send them on their own.

The fairies did not command the creatures of the forest, as such, but could make their desires for peaceful coexistence known to all sentient creatures. Nor did the fairies believe that any creature, including themselves, had a right to kill another, even for food. Therefore, all the forest inhabitants relied on fruit, nuts, lichen, mushrooms and nectar for sustenance. The fairies had a special relationship with a certain tree which grew in abundance and would, in the end, be their savior.

The Linga Tree

While the fairies lived on the ground and took to the air on occasion to reach the highest flowers for their nectar, they did not give birth in either. For this solemn rite a fairy about to give birth would build a nest in a Linga tree and wait for the birthing time. This had been so for many years, so many that none alive could recall why it must be. Nevertheless, when the time came, the urge to nest in the Linga tree was far too powerful to resist. This tree also provided the bulk of the fairies' food as it fruited year-round and bore a nut, called the Linga nut, which consisted of a soft, green husk on the outside and a small highly nutritious seed on the inside. The husk could be easily parted to allow the nut to be removed.

The Elves

One day, as the creatures of the forest went about their daily affairs, the fairies sensed a nearby but unfamiliar presence. It was upsetting because the pictures they saw in their minds conveyed hostility, something seldom seen in their world. A sense of foreboding filled the minds of the fairies and, in turn, was felt by the other creatures, too. A few of the fairies took to the air to scout this potentially harmful interloper. They discovered a band of elves riding on strange creatures known as horses. The horses seemed confused when their minds first saw the fairies' pictures but soon settled down when their peaceful intent was recognized. The fairies, however, saw in the horses' minds what the elves intended. They seemed to be a race of conquerors, searching for new lands to occupy and use for their own greedy purpose. The fairies sent pictures to the minds of the elves but they either didn't comprehend or just didn't care. In any event, their army continued on into the realm of the fairies. Their intentions were soon to become clear.

The Song of the Fairies

As the elves continued their march into the forest, they began killing some of the small furry creatures who lived therein and devoured them with great relish. Their desire to conquer and dominate was clear in the minds of the fairies. As one they took to the sky and began to sing. This was the purpose of their voices as the elves soon discovered. All at once the elves began to slow and soon dismounted to sit on the ground or a nearby rock. They experienced a peaceful calm that none of them had likely ever known. It was at once pleasant and unnerving. If an enemy could perform such magic, what else might they be able to do? At any rate, they certainly were not in the mood to make war. The fairies then began to send their pictures in an effort to explain the ways of the forest to the elves. If they wished to remain there were traditions to be honored. They may build houses but not from the wood of the Linga tree. They may eat the local flora but animals were not to be used for food. If they did not agree then they should be on their way.

The elves, having now regained their senses, spoke among themselves and decided that this land had much to offer so to remain, at least for a time, would be wise. And so, they agreed but things were not to remain peaceful for long.

The Kings Horde

Eventually word of the fairies' paradise reached the ear of the king. This king was even more greedy than the elves, and he decided to send his most powerful army to conquer it. These were human but had been bred, through several generations, to be blindly obedient to the king. This training and inbreeding had, of course, led to men of inferior mental capacity. They were fierce warriors who followed orders without thought to consequence or their own well-being. Once they were dispatched to the land of the fairies there was only one thought in their feeble minds-kill.

When the horde neared the land of the fairies there was mass confusion. The pictures the fairies received were cloudy and disjointed. They could, however, detect the horrifying nature of the invaders' intent. They called upon the elves to ask their thoughts about the newcomers. The elves had heard of a secret army under command of the king, but could offer nothing specific. The fairies, sure of impending disaster, asked if there might be a way to defeat them. The elves replied that if the fairies sang their song to appease the horde, the elves would not be able to fight. Without that advantage there could be no hope of defeating the beasts and saving the land. The fairies believed they had a solution and begged the elves to help save their home.

The First Linga War

The elves gathered in the shade of a Linga tree to hear the fairies' plan. It was simple, really. The elves, whose ears were quite large, were to put the fruit of the tree into their ears. In this way, the fairies could sing without weakening the elves' resolve, thus allowing them to fight.

This was done and the elves confronted the king's army before they had entered the forest. The song of the fairies had slowed the creature but, due to their limited mental capacity, they were still ferocious. The battle rage for many days and the elves suffered some losses despite the efforts of the fairies. In the end, however, the horde was defeated and the creatures of the forest went about cleaning up what was left of them. Meanwhile, the fairies heaped praise upon the elves and shared in their grief at the loss of their fellows. They were truly now part of the forest family and would always be welcome. Slowly but surely peace returned to the land although none would ever forget what had transpired. It never became clear whatced the king thought when his army did not return.

The Second Linga War

Peace had returned and the creatures of the land slowly returned to their everyday lives as they had been before the invasion. The elves, however, did not have it in their nature to leave things as they were. They were, after all, nomadic creatures who were born to conquer. Being under the spell of the fairies had never set well with them but they had been given little choice-accept things as they are or move on. But the battle with the horde had given them an idea. The fairies had sung while the battle raged and the elves had not been affected. Wouldn't that finally afford them a way to conquer this land as they had intended?

The elves went about gathering the fruit of the Linga tree and placing the green husks in their ears. When all was ready, they began to hunt down the fairies in order to force them to cede their homes to the elves. The fairies, of course had seen the pictures in the minds of the elves right away. They intentionally waited until all the elves had inserted the Linga nuts into their ears, then took flight as one and flittered about high above the forest. The elves believed they were trying to escape and were determined to wait them out; after all, they couldn't stay up there after dark.

Once the fairies were all airborne, they began to sing. This was a different song, however, than the one used against the king's horde. This was a very high-pitched wail that was piercing and shrill. Suddenly all the Linga nuts in the elves' ears burst open, driving the nut deep into the brain. The entire population of elves fell dead where they stood as the song of the fairies faded. Having violated their own sacred oath, the fairies would mourn their actions for many years and the story would be passed on to future generations. As necessary as it had been to defend themselves, the fairies were deeply troubled by what they had been forced to do. Meanwhile, the other creatures of the forest busied themselves once again cleaning up the mess of war.

Today the fairies still recount the story of the Linga Wars but continue to treat strangers as friends unless they should prove otherwise. If you happen to visit the land of the fairies, be on your best behavior; they have many songs to sing.

The End

Made in the USA
Middletown, DE
01 May 2024

53657972R00176